W9-BMO-634

MICHIGAN'S PERE MARQUETTE RIVER

PADDLING THROUGH ITS HISTORY

DOC FLETCHER

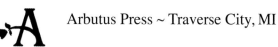

Arbutus Press ~ Traverse City, MI

Michigan's Pere Marquette River: Paddling Through Its History ©2013 Doc Fletcher

ISBN 978-1-933926-51-3

Arbutus Press
Traverse City, Michigan

Kite Aerial Photography by Juan N. Only
 www.juannonly.com
In Kite Aerial Photography, a camera is mounted in a rig which hangs from the kite line. The kite is then used to lift the rig into the air for some low-level aerial photographs. The rig can be very simple, in which the camera is in a fixed position within it, or more complicated with servos that change the pan and/or tilt orientations of the camera. The servos may be controlled automatically by electronics on the rig or through radio control (RC) from the ground. The triggering of the camera shutter can be through automatic circuitry internal or external to the camera (such as an intervalometer) or by a servo that presses the shutter button.

Photographs: Doc Fletcher, Juan Shell, Paul "Colonel" Braun, John Parsons
Maps: Maggie Meeker
Illustration: Keith Jones, Bigtimeartguy.com
Book design: Susan Bays, Fetching Design

Printed in China

CONTENTS

ACKNOWLEDGEMENTS

To Maggie, always loving, always supportive, always making me laugh.

To Baldwin Canoe Rental for providing the excellent canoes 'n kayaks, and getting us and our gear where it all needed to be.

To Barothy Lodge, Michigan's finest hideaway, for serving as an excellent base of operations and providing beds after our days on the P.M.

To Maggie and Toni for fueling the paddlers, cooking like Aunt Bee expecting company on Christmas morning.

To Jonesey, aka bigtimeartguy, my 4Day brother, for the wonderful art.

To Frank Lary, the great Detroit Tiger pitcher of the 50s and 60s, for being the "Yankee Killer", including an incredible 13 and 1 against the Bronx Bombers in 1958 and 1959 combined. This has nothing to do with canoeing and kayaking, but it sure is nice to think about.

To our paddling friends, aka the crack research team, for their keen observations, wisdom, laughs and camaraderie on the river.

DEDICATION

To Marquis and Chucky, dear brothers and fellow paddlers.

To my father, Herb Fletcher.

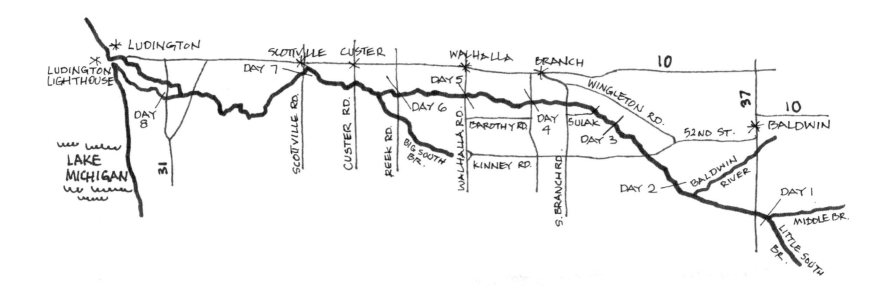

THE PERE MARQUETTE RIVER

INTRODUCTION

The Pere Marquette River, known to many as the P.M., is the mid-state boundary holding together the northern and southern halves of Michigan. It is the Great Lakes State river highway where north meets south, a state of Michigan designated Blue Ribbon Trout Stream & Natural River, and a federally-designated Wild and Scenic River.

If you love canoeing and kayaking you will love your time on the P.M. A day on the river features a current with above-average speed, steering challenges through and around its fallen trees and hanging branches, gorgeous driftwood, and among its abundant wildlife are majestic blue herons flying just ahead of you. A journey down the Pere Marquette is wonderfully wide-open as the P.M. is the only major river in the Lake Michigan watershed that flows unimpeded by a dam.

The 65-mile long Pere Marquette River runs through the Manistee National Forest. Located in the northwest section of Michigan's Lower Peninsula, the river flows from east to west, roughly parallel and south of US10. Its headwaters form southeast of Baldwin, at the confluence of the Middle Branch and the Little South Branch, a place called "the Forks". From there it winds its way westward by the towns of Baldwin, Branch, Walhalla, Custer, and Scottville until the P.M. empties into Lake Michigan a few feet south of the lighthouse in Ludington.

The majority of the P.M.'s riverbanks are privately-owned, but there are 18 well-maintained public access points on the river, from the Forks in the east to the Father Marquette Memorial access at Ludington in the west. At 4 of the 18 access sites there is camping available: Gleason's Landing, Bowman Bridge, Sulak, and at Henry's Landing. A 5th Pere Marquette riverside camping area is a free "canoe-to-only" campsite known as Elk, 10 minutes downstream from the Upper Branch Bridge. Although not a canoe/kayak access, a 6th riverside campsite is at Claybanks, located between the Green Cottage and Gleason's Landing access points. All public accesses and campsites are listed in the back of the book.

This book breaks the 65 miles of the Pere Marquette River into 8 paddling day trips. Each of the day trips gets its own chapter. The day trips range in miles from 5 to 12, and range in hours from 2 to 4. Each chapter lists the miles and hours for that day trip, directions to its starting access point, a day trip overview and a river map outlining the day trip from start to finish. Key landmarks are noted along the way to let you know how you're progressing against the trip's total miles and minutes. Also included is a "degree of difficulty" canoeing & kayaking rating for that day trip, a simple 3-step rating: 1. Beginner, 2. Intermediate (the difference vs. beginner is "can you steer around obstructions or through fast water?") and 3. Skilled.

Chapter 1 puts you on the river at its beginnings, near Baldwin. From there each subsequent chapter takes you further and further west, until the river flows into Lake Michigan in Ludington at the end of chapter 8. As you travel west, the fascinating history of the area will open up to you in sidebar articles, from the Idlewild resort just east of Baldwin, a special getaway where black vacationers were welcomed (while being entertained by Louis Armstrong and Sarah Vaughan) during segregation days, to Father's Marquette's death on the shores of Lake Michigan near the Pere Marquette's rivermouth, as he was trying to get back to his beloved St. Ignace. One of the historical sidebars, in between Idlewild and where Father Marquette took his final breath, tells the story of one of the last great Native American versus Native American battles in the Midwest, known as "Notipekago" and fought along the P.M. south of the town of Custer.

This is a paddling book, but any discussion of the P.M. would be incomplete without a mention of its world class fishing. The first recorded planting of brown trout in the U.S. took place in the Pere Marquette river system; fishermen are attracted in large numbers to the "flies only – no kill" stretch from M37 to Gleason's Landing; the river has an outstanding reputation as an anglers' paradise for steelhead, wild Chinook (King Salmon) and brown trout. One of the most beautiful sights you'll see while canoeing or kayaking down the P.M. is that of a fly fisherman standing midstream in knee-deep water, making that big loop with his or her line, before sending it across the water in search of the next fish.

The P.M. is a treasure and, as Michigan residents, we are fortunate to have living among us a group of people dedicated to keeping this treasure as pristine and unimpeded as possible, the Pere Marquette Watershed Council. Founded in 1970, the PMWC is one of the oldest local conservation groups in the country. Their many successful protective and restorative projects include minimizing riverbank erosion, thwarting the building of dams on P.M. tributaries (thus avoiding the warmer waters which would degrade fishing on the entire river system), providing aquatic research and research funding, and improving water quality and fish habitat.

Public service announcement: while you're traveling in the Pere Marquette River area, you can keep track of the Detroit Tigers by turning the radio to 97.3 FM.

Let the P.M. put an imprint on your soul,

Doc

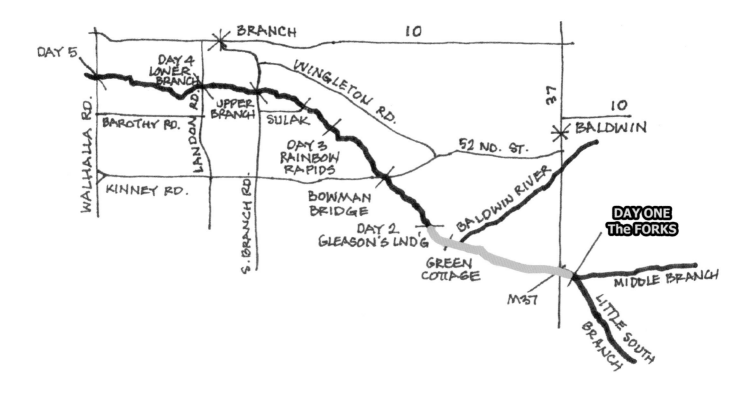

Launch directions: to the Forks - from Baldwin, take M37 South for 3 miles (passing Baldwin Canoe Rental) to 76th Street and turn left (east). Take 76th east for one-half mile, passing over the Little South Branch, to James Street and turn left (north). The Forks access will be on your left in .2 of a mile. The access has toilet facilities.

PERE MARQUETTE RIVER – DAY ONE

The Forks to Gleason's Landing
9.5 miles, 2 hours 56 minutes
Suggested Paddling Ability: Intermediate

River quote: "The thing about quotes on the Internet is that you cannot confirm their validity" - Abe Lincoln

Soundtrack: Mood Indigo – Duke Ellington, Growing Older But Not Up – Jimmy Buffett, King of the Road – Roger Miller, My Hair Had a Party Last Night – Trout Fishing in America, Big John – Jimmy Dean

Day One Overview: the Forks is the very beginning of the Pere Marquette River, where the Little South Branch and the Middle Branch merge to form the P.M. Day One takes you through a shallow and mostly sandy riverbed with a depth that varies from 6" to 3' deep, and a width from 20' to 50'. Flies Only – No Kill! is the fishing policy from M37 to Gleason's Landing. The impact of this on the fish population was evident during a September visit, as salmon filled the entire width of the P.M. at the M37 Landing. There are plenty of Day One deadwood challenges, and fine rapids runs a little over 1 hour and again 2 hours in, requiring steering skills beyond that of a beginner. Halfway into today's journey, a little over 90 minutes from launching, is an excellent break location with toilet, picnic table and marked by a "Rest Stop" sign. Two hours in and on your right, you arrive at Claybanks where it's too steep to serve as an access point but where a hillside stairway can take you to campsites and restrooms not visible from the river.

Day One in Miles and Minutes:

.4 miles/9 minutes: As the P.M. bends left, a creek merges right. James Road will soon be on your right.

.9 miles/20 minutes: a right bank sign tells you that the fine hillside log cabin you see is within the "Shrine of the Pines", Baldwin home to over 200 white pine creations built between the 1930s to the 1950s by Bud Overholzer.

The 1 mile break with Roger Miller: I smoke old stogies I have found, short but not too big around. Q: Mister Umphrey, are you a man of means? A: By no means. But he is the King of the Road.

1.1 miles/24 minutes: The M37 Landing, with toilet facilities, is on your left. The M37 highway is visible in the distance. Immediately beyond the highway homes & cottages are seen frequently along the riverbanks.

1.8 miles/39 minutes: Paddle beneath a railroad bridge. 5 minutes downstream, the rail bed sits upon a high ridge on your left as the P.M. turns to the right, letting you know that you are exactly 2 miles into the trip.

2.1 miles/47 minutes: As the river bends right, a large white lodge sits on the river elbow along the left shore, its porch looking down on the P.M. from a 50' tall bluff. This is the home of the Flint Rainbow Club.

3.1 miles/1 hour 7 minutes: A goiter on the river's elbow – as the P.M. turns left there is a large water basin on your right. A fine looking A-frame sits upon the right ridge.

3.2 miles/1 hour 9 minutes: The yellow A-frame on the right signals the start of whitewater, a 2-minute/3-bend long class 1 rapids run.

Salmon on river bottom at M37 access

3.4 miles/1 hour 12 minutes: On the right bank, a fish profile sign fronts a rustic cabin and outhouse. The boats glide over a bed of stones below the surface, with occasional larger rocks 2' to 3' in diameter. Blue Herons fly around the next river bend. Downstream one minute on a left ridge sits the brown cottage where Jimmy Dean lodged while fishing Chinook for a March 1983 "Outdoor Life" TV documentary. Jonesey noted the faint smell of sausage as we canoed by.

3.8 miles/1 hour 19 minutes: Baldwin River merges from the right. At this junction, both the P.M. and the Baldwin River are 30' wide and 2' deep. The P.M. quickly widens to 50' from the extra volume of the Baldwin River.

4.1 miles/1 hour 25 minutes: "U.S. Forest Rest Stop 15 Minutes Ahead" sign on the left.

4.8 miles/1 hour 37 minutes: The Rest Stop sign on the left shore marks a fine location to beach the boats and stretch your legs. Parallel to the river, a long wooden walkway ends at steps which take you up to a toilet, a picnic table, and a great elevated view of the Pere Marquette.

5.1 miles/1 hour 45 minutes: The Green Cottage access is on the left. The sign here reads "2 hours until next landing". That next landing is Gleason's Landing, only 1 hour 15 minutes away during our springtime paddle.

6.2 miles/2 hours: Beautiful wooden steps rise steeply up the side of a right bank hill to Claybanks, a campground not visible from the river. The P.M. turns to the left as it flows around a small island.

6.6 miles/2 hours 5 minutes: class 1 rapids take you on a wild ride through a boulder-infested, 2-minute long, rock garden.

7.7 miles/2 hours 22 minutes: On the left, a footbridge crosses over a merging creek. One minute later, a fast-flowing creek enters the P.M. from the right.

8.2 miles/2 hours 33 minutes: An excellent break spot is at the dirt beach on a right bend.

8.8 miles/2 hours 42 minutes: On the right side hill, stairs lead up to a stone wall. There is no home visible from the river.

9 miles/2 hours 45 minutes: Paddle beneath telephone/power lines.

9.2 miles/2 hours 49 minutes: 17 footings peak above the water line left of midstream, easy to paddle around.

9.5 miles/2 hours 56 minutes: You are in! Gleason's Landing is on the right.

THE FORKS TO GLEASON'S LANDING CRACK RESEARCH TEAM:

Perry VerMerris, Jim Mackza, Johnny Steck, Kenny Umphrey, Gus Weaks, Chris Weaks, Paul "Mister P" Pienta, Keith "Jonesey" Jones, Doc

Sources: John & Jay at Baldwin Bait & Tackle, Jeff Beilfuss at Baldwin Canoe Rental

IDLEWILD

Idlewild where back in the day it was said, "the men are idle and the women are wild!"

Imagine it is summertime in the 50s and you're driving through northern Michigan. As you draw near to Baldwin, you turn down the Tiger game on the radio and begin to hear a song echoing through the woods...

> *Folks, now here's the story 'bout Minnie the Moocher,*
> *She was a red-hot hootchie-cootcher,*
> *She was the roughest, toughest frail,*
> *But Minnie had a heart as big as a whale*

Cab Calloway in northern Michigan? Oh yes, and in the 40s, 50s and 60s, not just Cab but also fabulous musicians like Sarah Vaughan, Duke Ellington, Count Basie, B. B. King, Dinah Washington, T-Bone Walker, Louis Armstrong, Sammy Davis and many others. They were entertaining folks just minutes east of Baldwin at the Flamingo and Paradise Clubs in the resort town of Idlewild.

From 1912 to 1964, Idlewild was one of the few resorts in the USA that welcomed non-whites. Located near the headwaters of the Pere Marquette River, and often referred to as the "Black Eden", Idlewild was the rare place in our country where Black America could enjoy a vacation and buy property. At the peak of its popularity, it was the top-drawing resort in the entire Midwest, with 25,000 folks coming to camp, swim, fish, hunt, and relax – when not grooving to the top musicians in the country.

"Duke Ellington taking the "A" Train to the folks at Idlewild.

Strangely, it was the break-though 1964 Civil Rights Act that began the decline of Idlewild. With the end of segregation days, non-whites now had a wide-range of options to choose from for spending their vacation dollars. More often than not those vacation dollars were spent at places other than Idlewild.

After a long period of stagnation, Idlewild today is making a comeback. Although not on the level of its halcyon days of the 1930s to mid-1960s, folks are being drawn back to the area. The local natural beauty could not be denied for long with its gorgeous forests and 3 pristine lakes. New small businesses have opened and the number of permanent residents is on the rise. People are coming back to enjoy the area's nature and events like the annual Idlewild Jazz Festival. Hi-de-hi-de-hi-de-hi

The Idlewild Historic Cultural Center shares with its visitors the fascinating story of the area. It is located 3 miles east of Baldwin and just south of US10 at 7025 Broadway Ave.

THE TOWN OF BALDWIN

The heart of Lake County is at the intersection of highways US10 and M37, which means that the heart of Lake County is the town of Baldwin. The town is 72 miles north of Grand Rapids and 61 miles south of Traverse City. It was established in 1870 as a lumber center and named after the man who was Michigan's governor at the time, serving from 1869 to 1873, Henry Baldwin. The county name is derived from the fact that it is home to over 150 lakes. Lake County also has within its boundaries some of Michigan's finest rivers, which means that it has within its boundaries some of the USA's finest rivers: the Pine, the Little Manistee, and the Pere Marquette.

Besides the great paddling, fishing and boating in the area, there's a wide-variety of other outdoor activities. The 56-mile long Pere Marquette State Trail has its trailhead in Baldwin, 1 block east of M37 and just off of 9th Street. From there, it runs east through the towns of Idlewild, Chase, Reed City, Hersey, Evart, Farwell and Clare. Peaceful and rustic, sometimes paved and sometimes not, the Trail runs on the former CSX Railroad line. It provides the traveler with fine vantage points overlooking the Baldwin (a Pere Marquette River tributary), Hersey and Muskegon Rivers. Whether on foot, biking, or snowmobiles, the Pere Marquette State Trail takes you through towns and tunnels, over bridges, and past woodlands, wetlands, and farmlands.

Separate from the Pere Marquette State Trail, Lake County has over 300 miles of groomed snowmobile trails and over 300 miles of ATV/OTR trails. One-half of the county is covered by the Manistee National Forest and the Pere Marquette State Forest, providing plenty of opportunities for hiking, hunting, birding, cross country skiing, paddling, camping, and wildlife viewing.

In 1972, while Billy Martin's Detroit Tigers were driving towards the American League East Division title (the name Woody Fryman brings a smile), 8 motorcycle riders gathered at Baldwin's St. Ann Catholic Church to receive a blessing for a safe and happy riding season. No one could have expected what developed from that late-May day. Annually, thousands of motorcycle enthusiasts now gather at 1PM on the third Sunday of each May for the "Blessing of the Bikes" at the airport on M37 just south of town. Bikes have been lined up as far away as 5 miles from the airport on that day. The Blessing has become a weekend long event in Baldwin. The town folk claim that this is Michigan's original "blessing", one often duplicated but never equaled.

salmon, and resident brown trout. The "fly water" extends from M-37 to Gleason's Landing.

We've established a tradition of renting a house or small cabin from the folks at the Pere Marquette River Lodge. They are gracious and helpful hosts, and we love our stays there every year. They also have fishing guides available to hire and inspire. They are a full service Orvis fly shop as well. Some years, when we feel our wallets growing thin, or when the Spring/Fall weather is especially nice, we camp at one of the National Forest campground sites. We especially like the Clay banks campground for its proximity to the fly water.

FISHING THE P.M.
CONTRIBUTING ARTICLE BY JOHN PARSONS

The Pere Marquette River is one of the great trout streams in America. It was the first river in the United States to host the German brown trout, which is now firmly established as one of the best game fish throughout the country. With the establishment of Pacific salmon and steelhead in the great lakes, the PM is also home to fantastic runs of these big trophy fish. I came to know the PM River through friends of friends, and we fish the PM twice a year: spring and fall. Our spring trips usually fall anywhere from Mid March to late April, while fall fishing occurs anywhere from mid September through October. We are primarily fly fishers, and the PM has a section of water known as the "fly water." In this stretch (7 miles of river) the regulations allow only fly fishing, and all fish must be released back into the river. It is a "no kill" stretch of great fishing for steelhead,

24

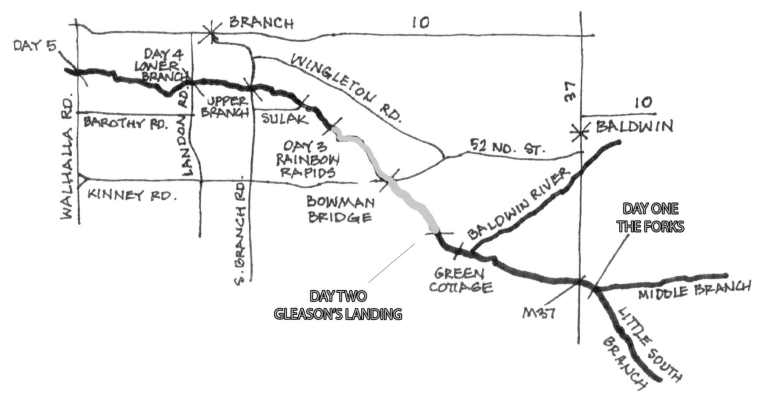

Launch directions: to Gleason's Landing - from M37 in downtown Baldwin, take Eighth St west for one-half mile to Astor Road and turn left (south). Follow Astor Road to the first right that you come to, 52nd Street. Follow 52nd Street west for 2 miles to S Jenks Road – there is a sign for Gleason's Landing just before 52nd meets S Jenks – and turn left (south) at S Jenks. In .4 mi you hit a split in the road. Take the bend right which puts you on to the aptly named Shortcut Lane. On Shortcut Lane in .4 of a mile you then arrive at a stop sign and turn right (west) on to 60th Street. In .3 mile turn left (south) at S Brooks Road and drive for one-half mile to the north banks of the Pere Marquette. Camping and restrooms are available here.

PERE MARQUETTE RIVER – DAY TWO

Gleason's Landing to Rainbow Rapids
10.5 miles, 3 hours 20 minutes
Suggested Paddling Ability: Beginner & (during last half hour only) Intermediate

River quote: "Never get on the canoe bus early & then leave it to go pee. You might get left behind" – 8 year old Gus Weaks

Soundtrack: Signs – Five Man Electrical Band, Ridin' and Jivin' – Father Earl Hines, Dang Me – Roger Miller, Way Back Home – Jazz Crusaders, Whiskey's Gone – Zac Brown

Day Two Overview: From launching to just shy of 3 hours in, Day Two is a very laid-back paddling experience, for the most part 1' to 3' deep and 20' to 30' wide. After passing by the Bowman Bridge access (camping & restrooms) a little over an hour in, the P.M. stays shallow while widening to between 60' to 80' with a sandy floor that makes for ideal Frisbee-throwing conditions. 2 hours from launch takes you past the private access at MacDougall's, where there's a dramatic narrowing of the river, and then the cabins at Cannon River Ranch. The final 30 minutes of Day Two requires a fair amount of paddling skill, featuring very fun and challenging multiple rapids winding around rocks and boulders.

Day Two in Miles and Minutes:

.9 miles/21 minutes: The P.M. wraps around a peninsula on your left where a home with a 10' wide stone chimney sits on a ridge.

The 1 mile break with Roger Miller: This river is sweet and so's maple surple, makes you wanna sing "Dang Me" high from the highest tree.

1.2 miles/27 minutes: The gray A-frame on the right signals the beginning of a series of beautiful wooden lodges sitting atop a ridge rising up to 80' tall. The 5th lodge features 4 decks, and each has a tree growing through the deck's center.

2.2 miles/45 minutes: The 30' wide river bottom is very sandy and 2' deep. There is open land beyond the riverbanks. A creek merges from the right.

2.4 miles/49 minutes: "Acorn Acres Club" is on the right, a fine log cabin with a stone chimney.

2.8 miles/57 minutes: Paddle beneath the 56th Street Bridge.

3.3 miles/1 hour and 5 minutes: the Bowman Bridge landing is on your left. This public access has restrooms and camping.

Downstream from the Bowman landing, the river flows through a beautiful deadwood field. The Pere Marquette riverbed has widened to 60' and is a shallow 1' deep. The peacefulness of it all has prompted my young canoe partner Gus to say, "If I had a pillow and a blanket, I could sleep in this river chair".

4.6 miles/1 hour and 32 minutes: You paddle through a great, sandy-bottom, Frisbee field. The river is 80' wide and 1' deep.

5.4 miles/1 hour and 46 minutes: The river here is 80' wide and 2' deep, as wide and shallow as a chain store music selection. The sandy and obstruction free river floor makes for a fine place to stop for a swim. At the end of a long straightaway is a house high upon a hill on the left. An island lies just beyond the house – the most direct route around the island is right. Railroad ties are embedded in the rise of a hill beneath the home on the left. There are beaver and turkey sightings.

6 miles/1 hour and 58 minutes: MacDougall's Ramp is on the left, a P.M. private entry point that requires an access fee. Paddling through the MacDougall property on the left bank, you pass by a fine looking deck jutting out over the river, 2 brown cabins, and an impressive white lodge that was

formerly the base for guided fishing trips. The river narrows dramatically at MacDougall's from 60' to 30' wide.

6.2 miles/2 hours and 2 minutes: Beneath the telephone lines, the rivers widens to 50' as it flows through a sandy riverbed 1' deep.

6.8 miles/2 hours and 17 minutes: Cannon River Ranch begins at the left shore dock that stretches halfway across the river. The Ranch sits on a left bank peninsula and, within the property's 5 paddling minutes, you pass by two more docks, through two short and light rapids runs, and alongside the Cannon River Ranch cabins.

7 miles/2 hours and 22 minutes: Paddle below a pedestrian bridge at the end of the Cannon River Ranch grounds.

8 miles/2 hours and 44 minutes: A creek merges from the right. Looking down the creek you see a dam and waterfall on it. At the river-creek merger point, logs and wire impede creek exploration. Downstream pass by a small island and a high ridge on its right as the Pere Marquette turns to the left.

The rapids will take you home!...
8.8 miles/2 hours and 54 minutes: Nice class 1 rapids run winds around several bends.

9 miles/2 hours 57 minutes: Pretty birch trees on the left precede fun rapids running through a long and challenging rock garden.

9.5 miles/3 hours and 5 minutes: The P.M. bends right at an A-frame on the left signaling more rapids ahead.

10.2 miles/3 hours and 15 minutes: On your right, a thin finger of land extends into the river; on its point a dock and a fire pit sit in front of a home. Just downstream are class 1 rapids.

10.5 miles/3 hours and 20 minutes: You are in! The Rainbow Rapids landing is on the right.

The Gleason's Landing to Rainbow Rapids crack research team:
Gloria Weaks, Madelynn Weaks, Perry VerMerris, Jim Mackza, Johnny Steck, Kenny Umphrey, Gus Weaks, Chris Weaks, Paul "Mister P" Pienta, Keith "Jonesey" Jones, Doc

Sources: Jeff Beilfuss at Baldwin Canoe Rental

The Baldwin Canoe Rental

The Baldwin Canoe Rental is on M37, 3 miles south of the town of Baldwin. Renting boats, with over 400 in stock, for the Pere Marquette since 1968, they are Michigan's largest paddling livery. You name it, canoes, kayaks, 4-6 person rafts, and inner tubes are all available to rent.

Michigan has many passionate, knowledgeable, safety-conscious livery owners and none more so than Jeff & Patty Beilfuss and Jeff's Dad Roger at Baldwin Canoe Rental. BCR services the upper half of the Pere Marquette, from its headwaters in Baldwin at "The Forks" access to the Walhalla Road access. The trips range from 1 to 13 hours.

When the livery opened in 1968, it was located on the north side of Baldwin. Roger and Marcia Beilfuss started their canoe rental business in the old Phillips 66 station that they owned at the corner of US10 and M37. By the early-70s, they bought out Baldwin Boat & Canoe Livery and moved to their current location. Roger didn't canoe or even swim, but he and Marcia did know how to treat customers, and their business grew from 20 canoes in 1968 to over 500 canoes by the late-70s. During that time, Baldwin Canoe Rental serviced the Pine and Little Manistee Rivers, in addition to the Pere Marquette.

Summer weekend overcrowding on the Pine and the P.M. prompted the Forest Service to institute a permit system in 1980 on those 2 rivers. The permit system successfully reduced the July & August weekend overcrowding on the extremely popular P.M. stretch from the M37 Bridge to Bowman Bridge, and it introduced paddlers to other great areas of the river further downstream.

Jeff and Patty took over running the livery in 1992. Although Mom Marcia is no longer involved in the operations, you can find Roger anywhere from his easy chair in the rental office to driving the bus for a paddling group drop off or pick up. If Roger is transporting your group, his jokes and good humor will have you all laughing.

Rookies on the river can keep you laughing, too. Frequent questions that Jeff gets asked over the years include "which way do we go on the river?" and "does the river go in a circle so that we end where we begin?" One group of 4 gals rented a raft and then called the office on their cell to see if someone could come and free them from the rock they got stuck on.

Baldwin Canoe Rental is south of town at 9117 M37 in Baldwin, MI 49304. They may be contacted at phone number (231) 745-4669 or email sales@baldwincanoe.com. The BCR website is www.baldwincanoe.com.

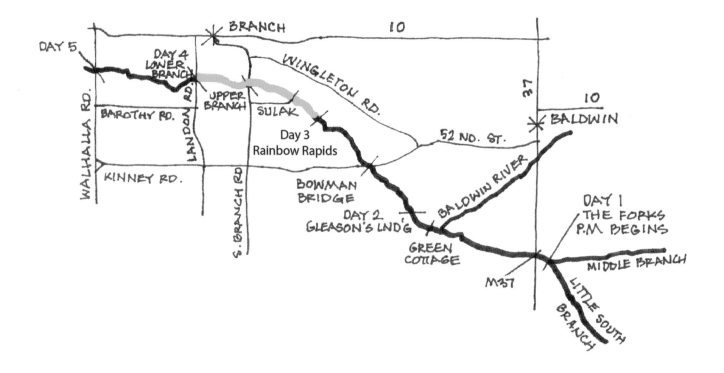

Launch directions: from M37 in downtown Baldwin, take Eighth St west for one-half mile to Astor Road and turn left (south). Follow Astor Road to the first right you come to, 52nd Street. Take 52nd Street west for 3 miles to the split with Wingleton Road. Follow the split to the right and on to the dirt of Wingleton Road. After driving for 4.4 miles and crossing over creeks twice on tree-lined Wingleton Road, turn left at the Rainbow Rapids sign and cross immediately over the railroad tracks. There is a restroom at the parking lot. Drive down the hill to the Rainbow Rapids access, on the north banks of the P.M.

Pere Marquette River – Day Three

Rainbow Rapids to Lower Branch Bridge
8.5 miles, 2 hours 43 minutes
Suggested Paddling Ability: Intermediate to Sulak, Beginner from Sulak to Lower Branch

River quotes:
"Where do you find a dog with no legs?"
"Right where you left him" – Kenny
Umphrey

"Paddling the P.M. at the start of trout season
ratchets up the challenge a notch" – Paul

Soundtrack: Rock the Boat – Hues
Corporation, 2,000 Pound Bee – the Ventures,
Do Wacka Do – Roger Miller, Look Out
For Deer – John D. Lamb, Beethoven's 5th
Symphony

Day Three Overview: This day features two distinctly different river trips: the first hour, from the Rainbow Rapids launch to the Sulak access, has plenty of rapids and paddling challenges. From Sulak to the Lower Branch Bridge takeout, you paddle through, except for a couple of fun light rapids near the day's end, quiet flat-water. Day 3 flows through a riverbed 6" to 4' deep and 30' to 50' wide.

Day Three in Miles and Minutes:

It's a wild ride right out of the chute!...
.3 miles/7 minutes: At the 2nd riverbend today is a fabulous class 2, boulder-infested rapids. Flying through here, Toni was knocked off of her seat (her toes pointed skyward, legs creating a "V" for Victory sign) and the canoe manned by Kenny & Jonesey flipped over. Kenny comes up with a new canoe rule: Yield to drift boats.

.6 miles/12 minutes: Paddle through light, class 1 rapids as the river bends left. On the right ridge is a wooden home with a beautiful stone chimney and deck.

.8 miles/19 minutes: The P.M. wraps around a pretty peninsula on the left. The setting includes a log cabin with storage house and a unique stone bird bath.

1 mile/23 minutes: Very enjoyable rapids rocket your boat through a rock garden.

The 1 mile break with Roger Miller: time for a little Do Wacka Do, both hands on the wheel and your shoulders rared back. Root-doot-doot-doot-doot, do-wah.

1.3 miles/27 minutes: WE.LYK.IT sign is on the front of the little A-frame on the right. Two minutes downstream a baby creek merges right as the river turns left.

1.5 miles/31 minutes: A sweet class 1 rapids hugs a peninsula on the left, running by a large number of A-frames.

2 miles/40 minutes: Paddle through class 1 rapids. Beyond the shoreline, a pileated, red-headed, woodpecker is busy at work.

3.2 miles/1 hour: The Sulak access is on the left.

Downstream from Sulak, the rapids are behind you and all is quiet water. The riverbed is 40' wide and 2' to 4' deep. Beyond the left bank are long, pretty views into lowland woods. High ridges with fine homes are on the right.

4.5 miles/1 hour and 26 minutes: The tiny home on the right looks like the perfect little hideaway, too small to require much upkeep.

5.4 miles/1 hour and 43 minutes: Upper Branch Bridge access is on the left. It features 2 side-by-side landings, the first for canoes & kayaks and the second for bigger boats. The "4 hours to next landing" sign refers to the Walhalla Road Bridge.

6.1 miles/2 hours: On the left bank is Elk, a canoe/kayak-in-only campsite (i.e. no vehicle access). Elk includes 4 sites, each with a fire ring and a bench, and an outhouse.

6.7 miles/2 hours and 10 minutes: Paddle through a one-minute long and very fun class 1 rapids. Gorgeous stands of birch cover the area.

7.5 miles/2 hours and 24 minutes: At a left bend in the P.M., an enchanting old weathered home is on the right. It's located just upstream from a fine Frisbee tossing area featuring a sandy pull-over spot on the left.

8 miles/2 hours and 35 minutes: On the right shore is a shaded, sandy beach, break area. A minute downstream is a small community of wooden cabins.

8.2 miles/2 hours and 39 minutes: A pretty little creek, 4' wide at its mouth, merges right. Just downstream is a 200 yard straightaway of class 1 rapids.

8.5 miles/2 hours and 43 minutes: You are in! Paddle under the Landon Road Bridge and exit the P.M. on the left bank dirt path at the Lower Branch takeout. As you walk your gear up the dirt path to Landon Road, watch out for poison ivy on both sides of the path.

The Rainbow Rapids to Lower Branch Bridge crack research team: Toni LaPorte, Kenny Umphrey, Paul "Mister P" Pienta, Keith "Jonesey" Jones, Maggie & Doc

Sources: Jeff Beilfuss at Baldwin Canoe Rental

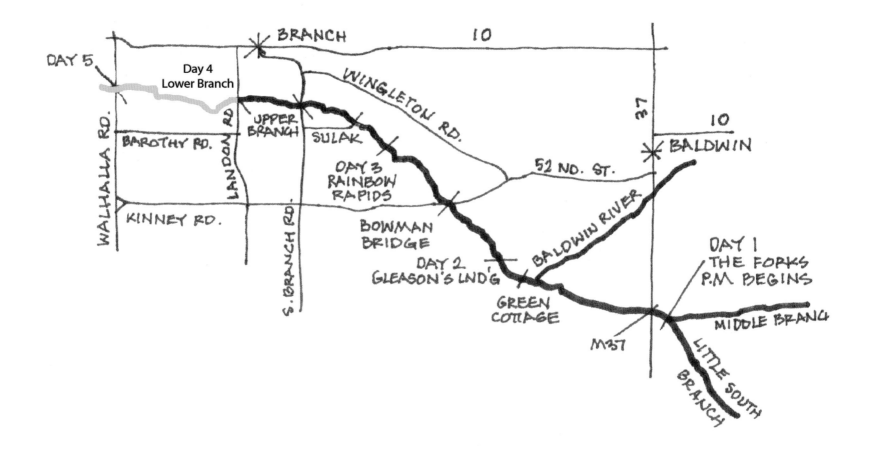

Launch directions: one-half mile west of Tyndall Road in Branch, and 3 miles east of Walhalla Road in Walhalla, is Landon Road. Take Landon Road south from US10 for .7 miles, and the access is just over the river and on the right (west) side of the road. There are no restrooms at Lower Branch Bridge.

Pere Marquette River – Day Four

Lower Branch Bridge to Walhalla Road Bridge
8 miles, 2 hours and 40 minutes
Suggested Paddling Ability: Intermediate

River quote: "The author dumped me! The author dumped me!" – Gilda Weaks

Soundtrack: Um, Um, Um, Um, Um, Um – Major Lance, Splish Splash – Bobby Darin, England Swings – Roger Miller, Boom Boom – Leslie West, Sneaky Snake – Tom T. Hall

Day Four Overview: P.M. Day 4 consistently features plentiful sightings of blue herons and gorgeous driftwood pieces as it runs through a, primarily sandy, riverbed averaging 2' deep and 40' wide. The rapids are light and enjoyable, while some of the deadwood encountered today challenges your steering abilities. There are a few deep pockets, or holes, where the river depth is over your head, but these are very few in number.

The Lower Branch Bridge to Walhalla Road Bridge crack research team:

Cheryl Orgas, Billy & Chris Meeker, Karen & Jeff Cripe, Gilda Weaks, Vid Marvin, Christine Verdone, Bruce & Pam Carroll, Laurie Zande, Billy Qualls, Maggie & Doc

Day Four in Miles and Minutes:

.6 miles/12 minutes: Steer around frequent trees and branches hanging down towards the river. The first high bank seen today, rising 60' above the shoreline, is on the right.

The 1 mile break with Roger Miller: Mama's old pajamas and your Papa's mustache, England Swings like our paddles do.

1.5 miles/32 minutes: Just before the river bends left, you're moving briskly through a pretty little rapids. Stay far left at the bend to safely pass by the "permanent" logjam.

2 miles/44 minutes: A nice sand break area is along the right bank facing a 70' tall sandy ridge on the left shore.

2.2 miles/47 minutes: on the right bank is a sign announcing the "Travers House".

2.7 miles/59 minutes: The "Logmark" sign on the right bank signals the halfway point of day 4. Not visible from the river, a well-hidden outhouse is located beyond the sign. Blue Herons are flying ahead of us.

3.3 miles/1 hour and 11 minutes: "Barothy property ends here" sign is on the left bank. You are at the upstream end of the Barothy Lodge land.

The Barothy sign signals the start of a fun, short rapids run through a deadwood field. Gorgeous fields of liatris are along both shorelines.

3.7 miles/1 hour and 20 minutes: At a midstream island, fast water flows right. A sandy break spot is on the right bank, facing a 60' tall bluff across the river.

4.6 miles/1 hour and 37 minutes: Paddling through the deadfall left of midstream takes you through a nice rapids run.
5 miles/1 hour and 43 minutes: The rapids run right of center. On your right, a spring cascades down a hillside to a rendezvous with the P.M.

5.7 miles/1 hour and 54 minutes: The "Barothy Lodge Canoe Landing" sign is on the left bank. The river here is 3' deep and 30' wide. 5 minutes downstream, at the foot of the Barothy Lodge Longhouse, paddle by the Ernest T. Bass Memorial Island, rumored to be a fine place to hide a still. At the Ernest T. Bass island stay left as there are plenty of obstructions blocking your way to the right. You will reach the downstream end of the Barothy property 15 minutes past the canoe landing.

6.9 miles/2 hours and 17 minutes: The Pere Marquette bends right at a nice island. A fast moving current flows around the island's right, where it's a challenge to maneuver through the deadwood. The open water is to the island's left.

Downstream from Barothy and on the approach to the Walhalla Road Bridge, the P.M. varies from 30' to 50' wide. Rising to a 50' high ridge, on the right bank you will see beautifully-decked A-frame homes and cottages.

7.5 miles/2 hours and 30 minutes: As you paddle beneath the power lines, you're less than 10 minutes from the Walhalla Road Bridge access.

8 miles/2 hours and 40 minutes: You are in! The Walhalla Road Bridge landing is visible ahead and on your left. There are restrooms but no camping at the landing

Day Four side note: "The author dumped me! The author dumped me!" Frequent paddling doesn't necessarily mean smart paddling. The river is always a good teacher - and a good reminder. Canoeing day 4 from the stern (back), I swung the front of the canoe to the right, perpendicular to the shoreline, to get an unimpeded photo of a midstream fly fisherman. As a result, my paddling partner Gilda and I were momentarily floating sideways downstream. Momentarily was a little too long today. A log sitting just below the P.M.'s surface met the side of boat – the exposed flank – and we were both in the river in seconds.

Never expose the side of the boat like I did, or be prepared for the possibility of an unfriendly meeting with what lurks below the surface. If you do flip the boat, stay calm and on the upstream side of the boat, to avoid the current rolling the boat over you. Start your river trip by securing all gear to the canoe/kayak cross bars with bungees or ties. That way when you pull the capsized boat to the nearest shore, all gear is coming with it. Keep a large ziplock filled with dry rice in your dry bag: once you're safely on shore, any electronics that get wet should have their batteries taken out immediately, and the device tucked into the ziplock with the rice. The dry rice pulls the moisture out of electronic devices. It's amazing how many cell phones, digital recorders, etc. have been saved this way on our river adventures.

1 Year below the surface – a gift emerges

The "Day 4" chapter ends with a side note, describing a canoe flipping, the result of the author concentrating on getting a photo of a midstream fly fisherman rather than paying proper attention to steering the canoe. A camera was thus lost on the P.M.

12 months later, on the morning of our dear brother Marquis' funeral (along with Chucky and my Dad who this book is dedicated to), I received a phone call from Jeff Beilfuss at Baldwin Canoe Rental. "Doc, did you lose a camera?" "Yep, a year ago, about an hour of paddling time upstream from Barothy Lodge" "Well, I think that we found it."

A few hours before this phone call, a family reunion at Barothy was wrapping up and two adult brothers took one last river tube trip before packing for home. When they entered the P.M. at the Barothy Landing, one of them saw the sun glistening off of something on the bottom of the river. It turned out to be a pretty beat-up camera. The camera was no longer functioning, but the memory card was in good shape. They inserted the memory card in their camera, which turned out to be the same make as that of the found camera, and saw photos of people standing in front of the Baldwin Canoe Rental van, getting ready to paddle the P.M. The brothers called BCR, described the people, and Jeff figured it was our paddling group and gave me a call.

"Something" prompted the brothers to take one last tube trip on what might be Marquis' favorite river behind Marquis' favorite getaway (Barothy) on the day of Marquis' funeral. We believed that the found camera and the returned photos – both believed hopelessly lost – was a gift from Marquis to his friends, letting us know not to worry because he's doing fine on the other side. Happening when it did, on the day of his funeral, allowed quite a few smiles to penetrate a day of sadness.

Marquis made his friends laugh time and time again with his spot on impersonations. His best impersonation may have been of the old Detroit Mayor, Coleman Young. One day, as Coleman was preparing to depart for a trip to Hawaii, a newsman asked the mayor if he had anything to say to the people of Detroit. Coleman answered, "Aloha mother f_____s". As funny as it was to hear the mayor say this, it was nowhere near as funny as hearing Marquis' version of this "Aloha mother f_____s" line. Knowing the Coleman Young story will allow you to better appreciate this story.

Jeff at Baldwin Canoes gave us the phone number of the brother who had taken the found camera home with him, so that we could arrange to get the memory card back. It was not an area code that we were familiar with, so Maggie looked it up. "You are not going to believe this" she said. "The first city listed under this area code is Aloha, Oregon".

BAROTHY LODGE

Michigan residents & visitors are blessed with many wonderful rivers and, separately, fabulous retreats deep in the state's great forests. If you're looking for the marriage of an excellent river adventure AND a special family/friend lodging getaway, arguably no single wilderness location does it better than Barothy Lodge. Barothy is located exactly halfway between the Pere Marquette River's Baldwin beginning and Ludington ending.

Situated within the Manistee National Forest, Barothy Lodge is a 320-acre resort with 15 beautiful rental lodges. The 11 largest each include their own hot tub, pool table, and fireplace. The resort sits along a 4-mile stretch of the P.M., and several chalets feature a stunning view of the meandering river. Paddling one hour downstream from the P.M.'s Lower Branch Bridge access, you begin to see Barothy's lodges.

The 4-miles of the Pere Marquette

that flows through Barothy's property is not only a great canoeing and kayaking stretch, but for fishermen it's paradise with some of the state's best runs of steelhead, salmon, and rainbow & brown trout.

You can spend hours hiking or cross-country skiing Barothy's well-marked forest trails, just a few minutes from the front door of your lodge. The amenities include a large fire pit, tennis courts, swimming pools, a half basketball court, climbing walls, volleyball courts, exotic bird viewing,

deer throughout the grounds, 4 stocked fishing ponds, and shuffleboard the way your grandfather played – at ground level.

Barothy Lodge gets its name from the man who built the first lodges on the grounds, Dr. Barothy. The doctor immigrated to the USA from Hungary, set up a practice in Chicago, and in 1889 purchased 65 acres of land along the Pere Marquette River. Previously this land had held the largest logging camp in the area, but Dr. Barothy saw its value as a health spa (spas were very popular at the time) due to the mineral springs along the river. In 1915, he remodeled his farmhouse into what is now known as the Main Lodge. Soon other buildings were constructed including the Long House (built with the state's first indoor toilet north of Newaygo). Over time, adjacent property was purchased, additional buildings were added, and Barothy's focus shifted from a health retreat to the recreation nirvana that we know today.

To get to Barothy Lodge, take US10 to the town of Walhalla (between Ludington & Baldwin) and turn south at the Walhalla Road blinker. Travel 1.7 miles to Barothy Road and turn left. Follow Barothy Rd east for 1 mile to the Lodge sign on your left.

Barothy's address is 7478 Barothy Rd in Walhalla 49458, phone no. (231) 898-2340, & the website is www.barothylodge.com. Their email is barothylodge@carrinter.net.

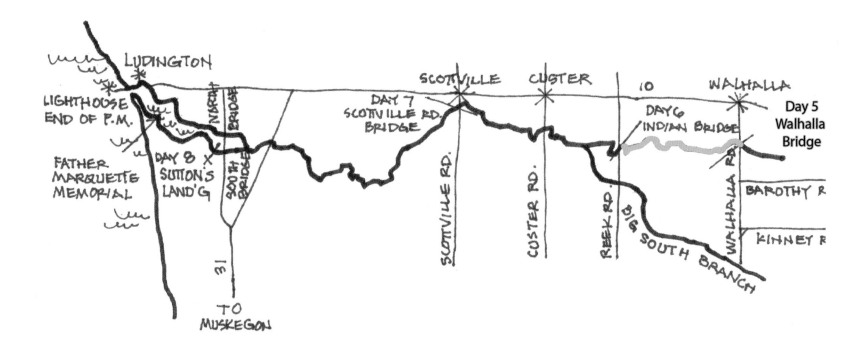

44

Launch directions: From M37 north of Baldwin, take US10 west for 16 miles to Walhalla Road and turn left (south). Take Walhalla Road for 1.4 miles, crossing the P.M. and turn right. There are restrooms but no camping at the access.

PERE MARQUETTE RIVER – DAY FIVE

Walhalla Road Bridge to Indian Bridge
5 miles, 1 hour and 42 minutes
Suggested Paddling Ability: Intermediate

River quote: "Where there's a will, I want to be in it" – author unknown

Soundtrack: Islands – King Crimson, I Can't Be Satisfied – Muddy Waters, My Uncle Used To Love Me But She Died – Roger Miller, Hungarian Rhapsody No. 2 – Franz Liszt, Tighten Up – Archie Bell & the Drells

Day Five Overview: From the Walhalla Road Bridge access, the P.M. is thick with cattails along and well-beyond the banks. Maneuvering around fallen deadwood presents a good paddling test. Threading the needle is required to make your way down this section of the P.M. Frequent cutbacks, back-paddling and tight steering is needed to find the narrow gaps among the river's obstacles. To paddle in the deeper river flow stay to the left (except where noted) of the many islands and splits. Almost 2 hours into day 5 are the memorable "Islands of the P.M.", a fabulous grouping of over 30 islands.

Day Five in Miles and Minutes:

.4 miles/7 minutes: Reaching the upstream end of an island, the main body flows left. It will take 8 minutes to paddle around the island. The Jonesey-Kenny canoe team break off to explore to the island's right (north) side.

.8 miles/15 minutes: Reach the downstream tip of the island. Jonesey and Kenny report that the island's right side is smooth sailing in the high water of springtime, but might be too shallow in "normal" summertime conditions.

As soon as you reach the end of the 8-minute long island, an 11-minute long island begins.

The 1 mile break with Roger Miller: My uncle used to love me but she died. A chicken ain't chicken 'til he's licken' good and fried. Keep on the sunny side, my uncle used to love me but she died.

1.4 miles/26 minutes: Paddle by the downstream end of the 11-minute long island.

1.6 miles/30 minutes: Come to a "T" in the river. The P.M.'s main body flows right. Whether you paddle right or left at the "T", the river reconnects in 1 minute. The water here is 40' wide and 3' deep.

1.9 miles/35 minutes: Gray home on the left bank has a Leinenkugel canoe sign on its deck, one of a series of homes sitting on the low left-bank ridge. Across the river are flat lowlands in front of a tall forest in the distance.

2.2 miles/42 minutes: An impressive landmark sits on a hill to your right, a gray lodge or mammoth home with big windows and a stone chimney.

2.4 miles/45 minutes: The river splits, moving in equal speed and volume (15' wide) both right and left, reconnecting in 1 minute.

2.6 miles/49 minutes: The river again splits, this time the main body flows left. The Jonesey-Kenny canoe team will explore the right split.

3.2 miles/58 minutes: The river reconnects from its 9-minute split. Jonesey-Kenny reported that the right (north) side of the split was flowing freely through gorgeous scenery. They did not reconnect to the main flow of the P.M. here: they had their own split on the river's north flow. Had they taken the left split, they would've reconnected with us at this 9-minute mark. Instead they took the right split and met us further downstream (at the 1 hour 5 minute mark). What they experienced by doing so: a very narrow stream thick with obstructions; they had to disembark from their canoe 3 times to pull it through the shallow water.

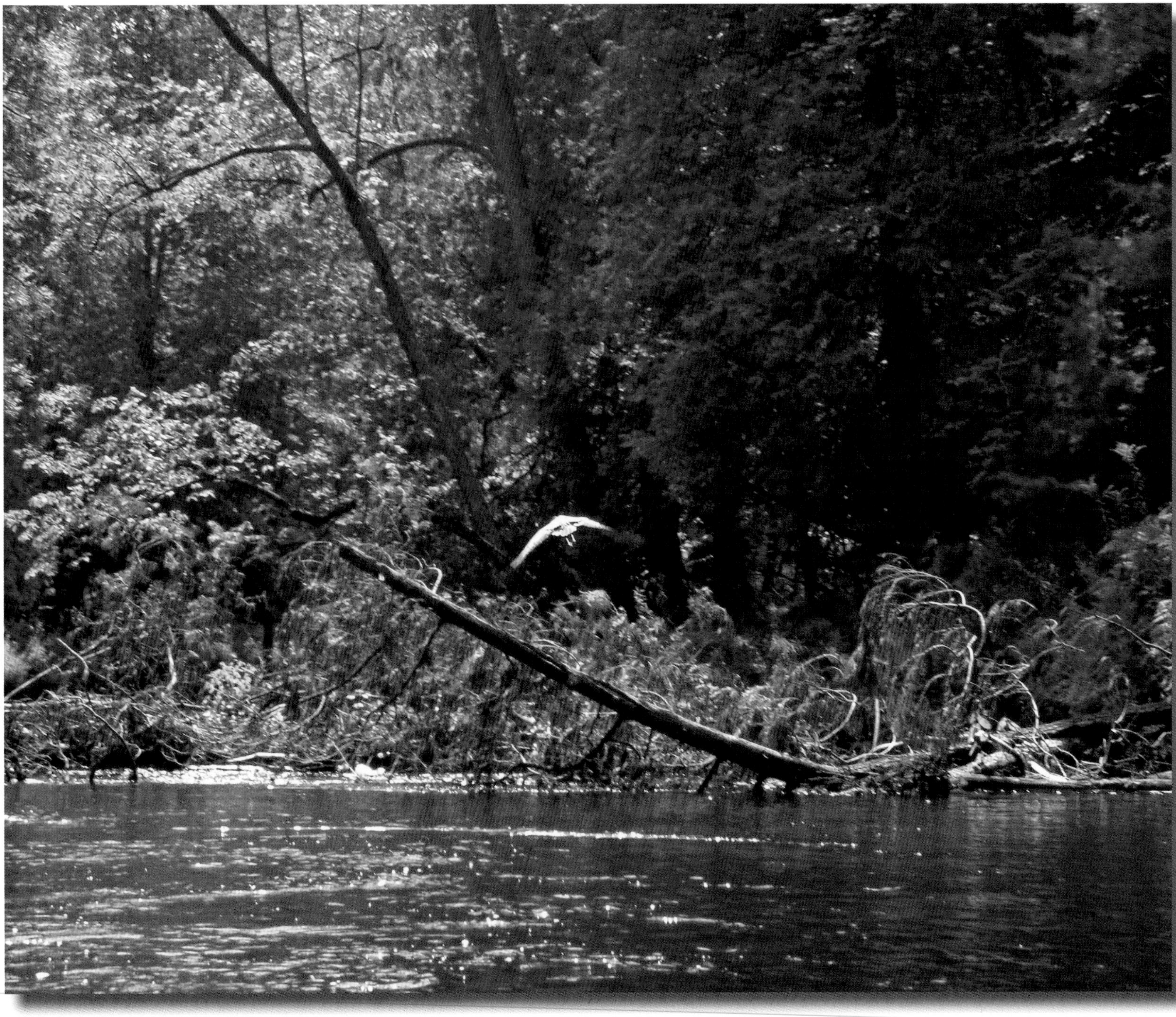

Beyond the P.M. split at the 3.2 mile mark, there are vast flatlands beyond both banks, stretching for hundreds of yards to high ridges of white pines, oaks and maples. There is a fine Frisbee field as the river flows straight through a riverbed 40′ wide and 2′ deep.

3.6 miles/1 hour 5 minutes: Arrive at a "T" in the river at the base of a tall ridge; a big home sits atop the ridge. The river and the Jonesey-Kenny canoe team, having been on a separate journey for 1 mile (splitting from us 49 minutes in) reconnect flowing in from the right. Turn left at the "T" to continue downstream.

THE ISLANDS OF THE P.M.

3.7 miles/1 hour and 7 minutes: It's a fascinating sight paddling through a neighborhood of over 30 islands ranging in length from 2′ to 100′. These are grassy islands, some with brush trees as tall as 30′. Canoe and kayak your way through one river split after the other. Follow the fastest flowing current for the best passage through the island town.

4.1 miles/1 hour and 18 minutes: A sandy and narrow strip of land where 3 fingers of the P.M. meet is one of the few good break spots past the Walhalla Road Bridge.

4.3 miles/1 hour and 24 minutes: At a big river split, go right. We went left at first, and then had to back out for lack of water. Arriving here signals the beginning of continuous river splits, or "spreads", through marshland. This is a popular bass and pike fishing area.

All of the river fingers will reconnect within 20 minutes, just before the take-out at the Indian Bridge access. This area is very shallow, no deeper than 6″, and may be difficult paddling in "normal" low summertime river levels. There is frequent deadwood and leaning branches to maneuver around and through.

4.8 miles/1 hour and 38 minutes: With the Reek Road Bridge visible through the trees, you can take any one of 4 river paths, and all will reconnect 1 minute before the take-out.

5 miles/1 hour and 42 minutes: You are in! 100′ past the Reek Road Bridge and on the left is the Indian Bridge access.

the Walhalla Road Bridge to the Indian River access crack research team: Kenny Umphrey, Paul "Mister P" Pienta, Keith "Jonesey" Jones, & Doc

Sources: Jeff Beilfuss at Baldwin Canoe Rental

NOTIPEKAGO

One of the last great area battles pitting Native American against Native American was fought along the banks of the Pere Marquette River south of Custer. Depending on the source, the battle took place sometime between the late 1600s and 1725. Over the years, stories of the battle have been passed down from generation to generation by word of mouth. Some details vary, but what is consistently told is that there was a terrible struggle between the Ottawa tribe and the Mascouten tribe, with deaths totaling in the thousands.

An estimated 3,000 Mascoutens were canoeing down the Pere Marquette, headed towards a friendly visit with another tribe further downstream. The attacking Ottawa surged into the water from both riverbanks. The fierce and bloody battle raged back and forth, spread from near the current location of the Custer Bridge to the west of it. The ambushed Mascoutens, unprepared for such a conflict, were eventually overwhelmed and all were massacred.

"Notipekago" translated means "place of the skulls" or "river with heads on sticks". The stories of why this phrase is used vary. One version says that all of the dead were buried next to the river shortly after the fight, but over time the shifting river uncovered some of the victims' skulls. Another story tells of victorious Ottawa who placed the skulls of the vanquished Mascoutens on sticks along the river's edge, as a warning to all others and to mark their supremacy in the area.

Tomahawks, arrow-heads, and knives have been unearthed over many years in the area, providing evidence of the great engagement that took place.

In 1840, in recognition of the Ottawa-Mascouten clash, the Michigan state legislature established the area of modern day Mason County as Notipekago County. 3 years later, the state legislature changed the county name from "Notipekago" to "Mason".

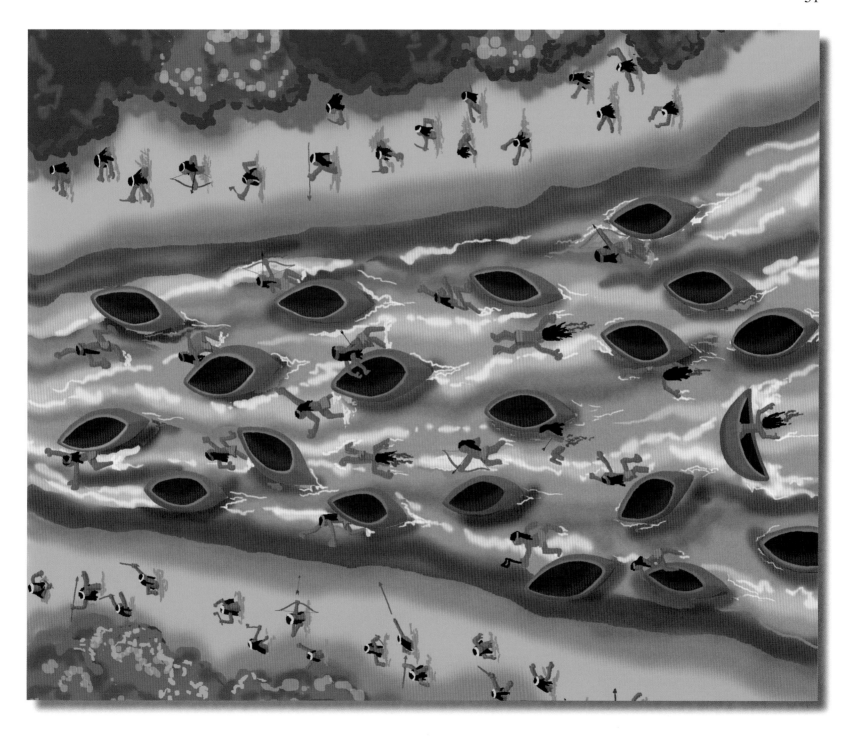

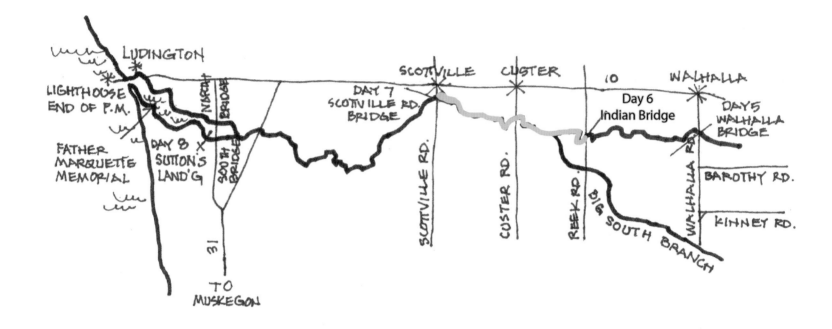

Launch directions: Reek Road is 3.2 miles west of Walhalla Road, and 2 miles east of Custer Road, at US10. Turn south from US10 on to Reek Road. Pass an asparagus farm in .6 of a mile on the right. At 1.2 miles south of US10, cross the bridge over the P.M. & turn right (west). The boat ramp is downstream from the bridge on the river's left (south) bank. Indian Bridge has restrooms but no camping. On the upstream approach to the bridge, the P.M. has 4 fingers flowing west, merging into one a few feet before the bridge.

PERE MARQUETTE RIVER – DAY SIX

Indian Bridge to Scottville Bridge
7.4 miles, 2 hours 45 minutes
Suggested Paddling Ability: Beginner

River quote: Doc "This is the longest undammed river in Michigan"; Maggie "I'm pretty sure that Jonesey damned it when his canoe flipped"

Soundtrack: Moonlight Fiesta – Echoes of Swing, Bohemian Rhapsody – Arrested Drunk Guy (Roger Wilkinson), You Can't Roller Skate in a Buffalo Herd – Roger Miller, Indian War Whoop – John Hartford, Midnight in Harlem – Tedeschi Trucks

Day Six Overview: Wonderfully relaxing best defines this section of the P.M. from the Indian Bridge to the Scottville Bridge. There is occasional bottom-scraping in the trip's first 20 minutes. Hills and ridges are the rarity today as it is flatlands to your left and to your right, viewed through a densely-populated forest. There are minimal fallen trees to paddle around and wildlife viewings are ample. Kick back and enjoy!

Day Six Miles and Minutes:

.1 mile/5 minutes: The Pere Marquette is 70' across and 3' deep. At the end of the first straightaway is the first of many river splits. The wider body of water veers left but you should stay right – even in the deeper springtime waters, we bottomed-out paddling left (i.e. summer trouble). Deeper water right, where there is also more debris to canoe and kayak around, is a consistent theme these first few minutes. To further the fun, many of the river splits each have their own splits as you paddle through a sea of islands.

1 mile/25 minutes: The river bends left at a grassy midstream island. Today's first hill is on the right, sandy and rising 25' above the Pere Marquette. The river deepens to 4' and widens to 30'.

The 1 mile break with Roger Miller: You can't roller skate in a buffalo herd, but you can be happy if you've a mind to. You can't take a shower in a parakeet cage…

1.2 miles/30 minutes: the Big South Branch of the Pere Marquette River merges from the left. The extra volume of the Big South Branch widens the P.M. from 30' to 80', and deepens the P.M. to 5'.

Within 3 minutes, the P.M. narrows to 60'. There are several blue heron and mallard sightings.

1.6 miles/40 minutes: A very slow-moving creek merges from the left. Two minutes later is a narrow and fast-flowing split to the left. A huge wetland is visible beyond the left bank.

2 miles/48 minutes: At the end of a straightaway, the river bends left at a tall, sandy hill. In two minutes is a junction with a dead creek on the right.

2.4 miles/56 minutes: The Custer Road Bridge access ramp is on the left, 20' upstream from the bridge. Paddling beneath the bridge, you're on a long and wide straightaway. The river is 3' deep and 50' wide.

From Custer Road to Scottville Road, the river depth will vary from 2' to 6' and width from 30' to 80'.

3 miles/1 hour and 10 minutes: At a right P.M. bend is a nice house on the left. Just before this a creek flows below a footbridge, the first of 3 merging creeks within 10 minutes.

3.6 miles/1 hour and 24 minutes: DNR "no wake" sign is on a left bank dock. There are plenty of turtle family sightings along the way.

3.9 miles/1 hour and 32 minutes: The best break spot today is a sandy beach on the right shore where the P.M. bends right. Just before the beach and on the left bank is a fast-flowing split moving away from the river.

4.4 miles/1 hour and 41 minutes: 5' wide finger splits off from the P.M. to the right, heralding the beginning of a series of river splits and merging creeks over the next 25 minutes. An increase in the amount of river deadwood requires no extra paddling skill and makes the journey that much more beautiful.

5.6 miles/2 hours and 7 minutes: The P.M. turns right where two homes sit on a low left bank ridge. 4 minutes downstream, a half-dead creek slowly merges on your right.

6 miles/2 hours and 15 minutes: the second great break spot today is the shaded sandy beach on the right, as the river bends right. 3 minutes beyond, another half-dead creek creeps in from the right. One minute downstream, 3 back-to-back-to-back fast flowing creeks empty into the P.M. from the right.

6.4 miles/2 hours and 24 minutes: A 30' wide & speedy creek enters the 50' wide P.M. from the right. The river at this merger is 6' deep. Two long creeks, one left and one right, flow into the P.M. over the next 3 minutes.

7.4 miles/2 hours and 45 minutes: You are in! After paddling through the Scottville Riverside Park and then beneath the Scottville Road bridge, the Scottville Road Landing is on your right, with restrooms. Directly across the Pere Marquette River from the landing is a fine riverside campground, Henry's Landing.

The Indian Bridge to Scottville Bridge crack research team:

Toni LaPorte, Katy Fritts, Tina Haley, Paul "Mister P" Pienta, Vid Marvin, Neal Linkon, Paula Brown, Donna Cooper & Juan Shell aka "Donjuana", Maggie & Doc

Sources: Jeff Beilfuss at Baldwin Canoe Rental, Josh Henry at Henry's Landing

Scottville Clown Band

Who says that there's nothing to do in Scottville on a Tuesday night? As we found out first hand, when the Clown Band is in town boredom takes a back seat.

The Scottville Clown Band was born 1903 as the Scottville Merchants Band. Back then, area merchants came up with the idea of dressing as hillbillies to entertain folks at local carnivals. Over time, as the band brought joy to a wider audience, their outfits became a bit more varied and colorful. The Merchants Band continued to entertain area residents until the demands of World War II resulted in the breakup of the band.

In 1947, the band was re-formed as the Scottville Clown Band. Town resident Ray Schulte (aka Mr. Scottville), whose father was one of the original 1903 group's founders, was the driving force in bringing back the band. Under Ray's direction they became a traveling outfit, spreading cheer to communities all across Michigan and beyond. As the Clown Band's schedule grew, so did their numbers. From a merry band of 14 in 1947, today the band counts 275 members. The once all-merchant ensemble now includes among their roster police, doctors, teachers, and lawyers.

Performing from their home in the Scottville Band Shell, you may hear the band play songs like "Jump, Jive & Wail", "God Bless America", "Tequila" (with maracas passed out to audience members asked to play along), and "The Lady is a Tramp". The songs are heavily salted with humor: when the guys got a little too enthusiastic while playing "The Lady is a Tramp", the director had to let them know that the lady is a tramp, not a prostitute.

On the group's tour bus is a coda that tells the band's story perfectly, "Thousands of miles… millions of smiles".

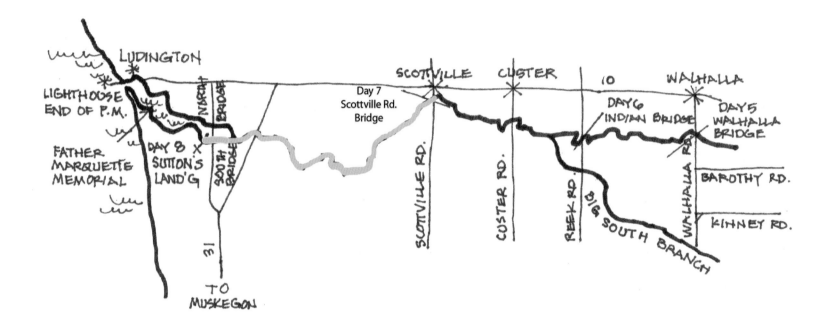

Launch directions: to the Scottville Road Bridge, from US10 in downtown Scottville, take Main Street south as it becomes Scottville Road. The P.M. is one mile south of US10. Just before arriving at the river bridge, turn right for the access. There is a dock and toilets at the access. Across the river is a second access at Henry's Landing and Canoe Livery, downstream and around the bend. Upstream from the bridge and on the left (south) bank is Scottville Riverside Park with docks, park benches perched over the river, RV park, swimming pool, & restrooms.

PERE MARQUETTE RIVER – DAY SEVEN

Scottville Bridge to Suttons Landing
12.4 miles, 4 hours 13 minutes
Suggested Paddling Ability: Intermediate

River quote: Colonel "Sometimes you reach a point in your life where things just tip over"

Soundtrack: Run Through the Jungle – CCR, Goodbye Stranger – Supertramp, Chug-A-Lug – Roger Miller, 25 Miles – Edwin Starr, Birdland – Weather Report

Day Seven Overview: A visual delight is what awaits you during the 4 hour journey from Scottville Bridge to Suttons Landing. Much of this section of the P.M. reminds you of the Spreads of the Fox River in the Upper Peninsula, as the river splits and rejoins – and the splits then split again - more times than can be counted. The splits reconnect as soon as in one minute and as long as in 90 minutes (the "parallel P.M.").

The finest wildlife viewing of the entire 65 miles of the river are here including bald eagles, mallards, hawks, turkey buzzards, deer, and a gorgeous sandy-hill bird sanctuary. The topography is primarily flat and seen through a thick jungle of trees, interrupted by the occasional ridge or hill. Midstream deadwood fields are at times dense and challenging, requiring paddling skills beyond beginner. This stretch of the Pere Marquette is an extremely enjoyable adventure.

Day Seven Miles and Minutes:

.5 mile/12 minutes: In the early stages today, the river runs an average of 50' wide and the depth varies from 6' (at launch) to 2'. At the half-mile mark and along the right shore a bald eagle is perched 50' above the waterline – the first of several eagles seen today.

The first of the river splits is at the .6 mile mark. They now occur with great frequency.

The 1 mile break with Roger Miller: Make you wanna holla hidy hoe, burns your tummy don't you know, chug-a-lug, chug-a-lug.

1.1 miles/27 minutes: 5 river fingers (splits) wind their way around a grouping of islands and rejoin as one – a memorable sight. 3 minutes later is a P.M. triple split and reconnect.

1.7 miles/39 minutes: The 1st ridge seen today is on the right. At its base is a lily-pad filled dead stream. One minute downstream a clogged, big creek merges from the left. A "Utopia" sign is on a left bank tree. The splits and reconnects continue.

2 miles/45 minutes: The swamp on the left lets you know you're 2 miles into the trip. 3 minutes later a "Paradise Found" sign is on a left bank tree. A long, wide, and slow creek empties into the P.M. from the right.

2.4 miles/54 minutes: On the right shore, a bird sanctuary populates the sandy hillside with hundreds of small holes where they make their homes. The birds emerge from these homes, blackening the sky above. It's a fascinating sight! The sanctuary is at the end of a long straightaway as the river bends left.

2.9 miles/1 hour and 3 minutes: "Attitude Adjustment Area" is suggested on a sign on a left bank tree.

The Parallel P.M. begins...

3 miles/1 hour and 6 minutes: There is a 20' wide right river split as the main body is 50' wide and moving to the left. Neal, Ron and Ronnie Jr. explore the right break, sending them on to the parallel P.M., a journey that will take them north and parallel to the main body for 90 minutes until reconnecting with the main flow of the river.
5 minutes into this parallel P.M. they paddle by a park marked by wolf and bear emblems and a foot bridge crossing the river. It is noteworthy that the parallel P.M. is sufficiently wide and deep, with gorgeous surroundings, to provide a fine experience.

3.2 miles/1 hour and 11 minutes: A "Serenity Zone" sign mellows out on a left bank tree.

3.5 miles/1 hour and 16 minutes: A long, dead creek connects to the river on your left. Left and right river splits follow. The left split takes you on a 7-minute journey before it rejoins the main river flow, widening it to 80' across. The river here is 2' deep. Deer race away from the shore as we paddle by.

3.9 miles/1 hour and 25 minutes: A beautiful and massive river birch hovers above the right bank. Mallards are everywhere and P.M. deadwood fields are now more frequent, enjoyably testing your steering skills as you thread those needles.

4 miles/1 hour and 28 minutes: On the left, 3 side-by-side-by-side creeks merge with the P.M. The 3rd one empties into the river by a small dock.

4.4 miles/1 hour and 37 minutes: A logjam stretches across the entire river. There is no portage required as you navigate through small gaps in the jumble of logs, creating a fun paddling challenge. Turkey buzzards are now our constant companions above.

5.2 miles/1 hour and 53 minutes: A home is beyond a left bank rise with a marshy alcove just upstream.

5.4 miles/1 hour and 58 minutes: There is a pronounced split in the P.M. with plenty of water flowing both left and right. 10 minutes downstream, the river is 30' wide and covered in a shaded canopy. At the right river bend a creek enters from the left where a small cabin is 10' from the river. The extra volume of the creek widens the P.M. to 70'.

5.9 miles/2 hours and 15 minutes: On the left, a road descends down a distant hill and leads to the river's edge. 1 minute later, at the 6 mile mark, a creek rolls in from the left at the base of a ridge.

6.1 miles/2 hours and 19 minutes: This is the beginning of a series of midstream, grassy islands, between 2' to 20' long.

6.4 miles/2 hours and 25 minutes: Two hills are on the left. A cabin with a stone chimney is at the downstream end of the 2nd hill. The string of grassy islands continues.

The Parallel P.M. reconnects…

6.7 miles/2 hours and 32 minutes: The Pere Marquette comes to a "T" at a huge junction as the big water – the parallel P.M. – merges from the right. It is at this point that Neal, Ron & Ronnie Jr. rejoin our group, after a 90 minute / 3.7 mile parallel P.M. journey.

7 miles/2 hours and 37 minutes: Big creek junction is on the left. A bald eagle swoops in low above the canoes and kayaks… very impressive. 3 minutes later paddle beneath the less impressive overhead lines.

7.6 miles/2 hours and 48 minutes: At a left bend, near the upstream edge of an island, the steep hill on the right is (artfully, not functionally) embedded with tables. The deadwood in the river is plentiful and, as the river is wide enough to maneuver around and through it all, it just adds to the P.M.'s joy.

8.9 miles/3 hours and 12 minutes: Big creek merges right. The P.M. is now 60 'wide and 6' deep, the deepest it has been since launching from the Scottville Bridge landing. Two minutes later, at the 9 mile mark, the river bends left at a nice red house on a right bank hill. There is another eagle sighting.

9.4 miles/3 hours and 20 minutes: Paddle below the US31 north and southbound lanes.

10.1 miles/3 hours and 32 minutes: A fast-moving split breaks off to the river's right.

Stay left at the "T"!...
11.1 miles/3 hours and 47 minutes: The river comes to a "T" at the upstream end of the P.M. "loop". For the next 35 minutes, the P.M. splits into the South Branch and the North Branch. Stay left (South Branch) for Suttons Landing, the Day 7 take out point. If you do paddle to the right, you will reconnect with the left branch .4 mile/ 8 minutes downstream from, or beyond, Suttons Landing.

As a side note, the folks at P.M. Expeditions tell us that it takes 2 hours to paddle around the entire loop (the North AND the South Branch).

11.7 miles/3 hours and 56 minutes: A fine break spot is at the left bank dirt beach as the river bends left.

12 miles/4 hours: Another excellent late trip break spot is a dirt beach on the right where the river bends to the right. It's a nice Frisbee location, too.

12.3 miles/4 hours and 9 minutes: The Pere Marquette Highway 31 landing is on your left, a very good access point w/o restrooms. One minute downstream, paddle below the Pere Marquette Highway and past the P.M. Expeditions Beers, Boats & Bait store on the left.

12.4 miles/4 hours and 13 minutes: You are in! Suttons Landing, complete with restrooms, on your left.

The Scottville Bridge to Suttons Landing crack research team:

Paul "Mister P" Pienta, Neal Linkon, Spencer Vollmers, Jimmy Vollmers, Eric Braun, Paul "Colonel" Braun, Ronnie Swiecki Jr., Ron Swiecki, Greg Palinsky, and Doc

Sources: Jeff Beilfuss at Baldwin Canoe Rental, Josh Henry at Henry's Landing, Pere Marquette Expeditions Beer, Boats & Bait

Ludington – the town once known as "Pere Marquette"

In the 1950s, Ludington had the distinction of being the largest car ferry port anywhere in the world. This position had its beginnings in 1897, when the folks at the Pere Marquette Railroad constructed an armada of nine railroad car ferries. The purpose was to allow the P.M. Railroad Co. to transport goods, primarily lumber, across Lake Michigan to serve the big city markets of Milwaukee and Chicago.

The origin of the Ludington that we know today was born 50 years before the Pere Marquette Railroad people built their big car ferry fleet. In 1847, a man named Burr Caswell decided that the perfect place to build his home would be at the river mouth of the Pere Marquette, where the river flowed into Pere Marquette Lake near Lake Michigan. Burr Caswell's home, cut out of the vast wilderness of giant white pines, soon grew into a small town that became known as the Village of Pere Marquette.

In 1854, little Pere Marquette Village was seen by one man as a fine location to build a sawmill. Needing cash to start this venture, George Ford borrowed the needed money from a 27-year old acquaintance of his from Wisconsin, James Ludington. By the end of the 1850s, George could no longer make payments on his loan, and his sawmill became the property of his financier, James Ludington.

What to do with a sawmill located across the lake from his Wisconsin home? James Ludington saw the wisdom in George Ford's vision and decided to expand his new holding, buying acres and acres of white pine. James put out the "now hiring" sign, and soon had several hundred men working at his sawmill. In 1867, James Ludington platted the Pere Marquette Village and started the area's first newspaper, the Mason County Record. In 1873, the village grew to 1,000 residents, was chartered, and chosen as the county seat. James offered to donate $5,000 to the citizens of Pere Marquette if they would rename the town after him. His offer was accepted, and the village once named after Father Jacques Marquette would now be named Ludington, after a man who never even resided here.

Although never a resident of Pere Marquette, later Ludington, James nevertheless was instrumental in encouraging the tremendous growth that the town experienced in the late-1800s. Besides creating hundreds of lumber jobs, James Ludington successfully secured state funding to expand the harbor, and invested his own finances to improve roads and bridges. Think of him the next time that you stand at the corner of James Street & Ludington Avenue.

Mason County Sports Hall of Fame

Located in historic White Pine Village is the Mason County Sports Hall of Fame. Created in 2004, the MCSHF celebrates those local area athletes who have made an impact on the sports world. Inductees include…

David Claire Not only was David the only person from Mason County to ever play baseball in the Major Leagues, but he accomplished this feat as a teammate of the great Detroit Tiger, Tyrus Raymond Cobb. The Ludington native was a standout shortstop for the Class B Ludington team, having a particularly strong 1920 season both at the plate and in the field. At the conclusion of that season, the Detroit Tigers purchased his contract and quickly put David in the lineup – hitting right in front of the supremely talented Ty Cobb. Although his play received fine reviews from the Detroit News, his days as a Tiger were brief. After 1920, David Claire never again played in the major leagues. The game was in his blood though, and his involvement in baseball continued for many years as a scout, a coach, and a manager at various levels for the Tigers, the Boston Red Sox and the St. Louis Cardinals.

Luke and Murphy Jensen Ludington natives, the Jensen Brothers were arguably the best-known tennis doubles team of recent times. Talented and colorful, the brothers won the 1993 French Open doubles title, were semi-finalists in the 1995 U.S. Open, and quarter-finalists in the 1994 U.S. and French Opens and in the 1995 French Open. All told, the Jensens won 15 Doubles Championships. Luke was known as "Dual-Hand Luke" for his ability to serve both left-handed and right-handed. Murphy claimed to be "the world's greatest tennis player that has ever lived… that grew up on a Christmas tree farm in northern Michigan… if you don't count my brother Luke". The brothers brought a breath of fresh air to the game, riding their Harleys, jumping out of airplanes, and entertaining at tour parties with their rock 'n roll band, "We've Never Heard of You Either".

Larry MacPhail A resident of first Scottville and then Ludington, few people had as much impact on Major League Baseball as Larry MacPhail. Along with Crosley Powell, he took over the Cincinnati Reds in 1933. In 1934, the Reds became the first team in any major sport to fly to away games. On May 24, 1935, the Reds played the first night game in major league history as President FDR threw the switch from our nation's capitol. Larry saw as his next opportunity the underachieving Brooklyn Dodgers. By 1941, he had the Dodgers in the World Series. Larry was smart enough to hire Red Barber as the Dodgers' announcer and Red broadcast the first televised Major League game on August 26, 1939. After a stint in the army during World War II, Larry became a co-owner of the New York Yankees before stepping away from the game in 1947. Larry & Lee MacPhail, another extremely successful Major League executive, are the only father-son members of the Baseball Hall of Fame in Cooperstown.

The Mason County Sports Hall of Fame and White Pine Village are located at 1629 S. Lakeshore Drive in Ludington MI 49431. Phone (231) 843-4808. Click on www.historicwhitepinevillage.org.

Ludington's Cartier Mansion Bed & Breakfast

Built in 1905 by lumber baron Warren Cartier, the neoclassical Cartier Mansion B&B is one of Ludington's historic treasures. It is an absolutely gorgeous bed and breakfast with a wonderful location, situated on US10 and a short walk east of the sparkling shores of Lake Michigan.

The mansion's creator, Warren Cartier, was elected Ludington's mayor in 1899 and re-elected in 1903. Energy, ambition, and success flowed through the family tree: Warren's father Antoine was also a wealthy lumberman and also twice elected Ludington's mayor (Antoine in the 1880s). Father and son's ancestor was the famous Frenchman Jacques Cartier who, through his 1534 and 1535 explorations of the St. Lawrence River and the Gulf of St. Lawrence, claimed present-day Canada for France.

Driving by, your attention is immediately drawn to the beauty of the Cartier Mansion's exterior with its' grand porch announced by 6 stately columns and immaculate landscaping and gorgeous gardens that wrap around the bed & breakfast. Although the view of the outside makes it seems unlikely, it's the interior that is even more spectacular.

Warren Cartier's original woodwork was stunning when unveiled in 1905 and has the same effect on visitors today. Every room was uniquely created in both their design and in the type of wood used. You enter through a foyer of white oak. The living room is rich cherry, the library (housing 1,000 books for guests) is black walnut, the music room is mahogany, and dining room sycamore. Each room's floors feature detailed inlays. The mansion also includes five fireplaces, each with unique imported tile, rare antiques, the original rugs, and chandeliers.

Besides these (anything but) common areas, are the five wonderful private bedrooms. The King Suite is the showpiece of the 5. Its big bedroom includes a sitting room and, in the spacious bathroom, the original 1905 cage shower and a Jacuzzi. The King Suite private balcony overlooks Ludington Avenue (US10) and when constructed in 1905, it was believed to be where Warren Cartier would give his acceptance speech when inevitably elected Michigan's governor (a position never realized by Warren).

The Cartier Mansion B&B has been owned and operated by Sue Ann and Gary Schnitker since 2005. It is located at 409 East Ludington Avenue in Ludington MI 49431. Their phone number is (231) 843-0101, website www.cartiermansion.com. You can also contact Sue Ann and Gary at garyandsueann@charter.net.

74

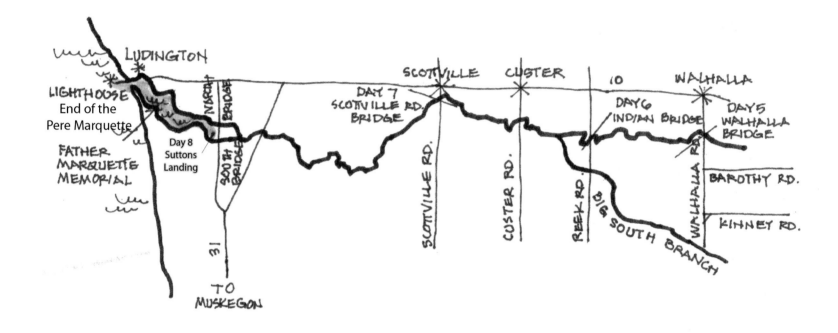

Launch directions: to Sutton's Landing – take US10 in Ludington to Pere Marquette Highway and turn south. Crossing over both the North and the South Branches of the P.M., it is 2 miles from US10 to Iris Road (at P.M. Expeditions Beers, Boats & Bait). Turn right (west) at Iris Road. In one-tenth of a mile, the entrance to Sutton's Landing will be on your right. It has restrooms, shelter, picnic tables, park benches overlooking the P.M., swing set, and a 200' long wooden walkway running parallel with the river.

PERE MARQUETTE RIVER – DAY EIGHT

Suttons Landing to Father Marquette Shrine/boat ramp via Ludington Lighthouse
5 miles, 1 hour 50 minutes
Suggested Paddling Ability: Skilled

River quote: Colonel (roller–coasting on the 4' high Lake Michigan waves) "Let's paddle over to the beach so I can clean my shorts"

Soundtrack: Michigan Coast to Coast – Brian VanderArk, Higher Ground – Stevie Wonder, Walkin' In The Sunshine – Roger Miller, I Want to Marry a Lighthouse Keeper – Erika Eigen, Sunset – Roxy Music

From Sutton's Landing to today's ending at the Father Marquette Shrine, turn right (west) on to Iris Road, taking it until it ends at South Lakeshore Drive, and turn right (north). Pass by the Historic White Pine Village and Buttersville Park (with its excellent campground overlooking Lake Michigan). The Father Marquette Shrine will be on your right, with the access behind it, on South Lakeshore Drive 1.6 miles from Iris Rd.

Day Eight Overview: In less than 1 mile from launch, the P.M. River widens into Pere Marquette Lake, where the car ferry S.S. Badger is docked between trips across Lake Michigan from Ludington to Manitowoc WI and back. On a calm day, the beginner paddler could traverse the P.M. River into P.M. Lake and take out at the boat ramp at the Father Marquette Shrine. Beyond here, the 65 miles of the Pere Marquette River comes to its end when relatively peaceful P.M. Lake meets the often times much rougher swells (4' high on our trip) of Lake Michigan at the Ludington Lighthouse.

78

Only life-jacketed experienced paddlers should continue past the Father Marquette Shrine in P.M. Lake to the lighthouse at Lake Michigan, a great adventure. You will turn around at the lighthouse and retrace your watery steps to the Father Marquette Shrine boat ramp, the only P.M. access downstream from today's Sutton's Landing launch site.

Day Eight Miles and Minutes:

.2 mile/4 minutes: While still in the P.M. South Branch section of the loop, you arrive at a field of pilings at the upstream end of a small island. Geese fill the sky. This is the great wilds of the P.M. The river is 50' wide and its depth varies from 2' to 6'.

.4 mile/8 minutes: The P.M. North Branch merges from the right and the loop, begun 35 minutes upstream, is now closed. Tall reeds and cattails are along both banks of the river.

.6 mile/11 minutes: Paddle beneath a footbridge.

.8 mi/15 minutes: The Pere Marquette River widens dramatically into Pere Marquette Lake. At this juncture there is a little island on the left with a sandy beach. During the first one-tenth of a mile into the lake, it is a shallow 6" deep with sand bars left and right.

The 1 mile break with Roger Miller: Think about a good time we had a long time ago, think about forgettin' about your worries and your woes, walkin' in the sunshine, sing a little sunshine song.

1.5 miles/32 minutes: On your right is the 2nd dock of an industrial island. The cross of the Father Marquette Shrine, high on a hill, is now visible directly ahead on the far western shore of P.M. Lake (to the right of a gray home with many windows). The S.S. Badger and the deactivated S.S. Spartan, twin car ferries, are docked in the distance to the north (your right). Although the winds today are only 5 to 10 mph, P.M. Lake is plenty choppy. Its depth is now well over the length of our paddles.

2 miles/43 minutes: Arrive at the boat ramp at the base of the Father Marquette Shrine aka "the Cross".

For experienced paddlers only…
3 miles/1 hour: Paddling north from the Shrine, and never straying over 100' from the west shore of P.M. Lake, arrive at the edge of a stone break wall. Turning left at the break wall, for the first time today, the Ludington Lighthouse comes into view. Paddling towards the lighthouse you are in the P.M. Lake channel on the way to Lake Michigan.

3.5 miles/1 hour 10 minutes: Arrive alongside the Ludington Lighthouse, the end of a 65 mile journey that began at the P.M. headwaters near Baldwin. The lighthouse is where the P.M. meets Lake Michigan, a chance to dip our paddles into the Big Lake. On this particular day, there were 4' high Lake Michigan rollers crashing against the base of the lighthouse. Turn around at the lighthouse, with the goal of retracing your steps and taking out at the Father Marquette Shrine boat ramp.

4 miles/1 hour and 25 minutes: With your back to Lake Michigan, a fine sandy beach is on your right, on the south side of the P.M. Lake channel. This makes an excellent break spot.

5 miles/1 hour and 50 minutes: You are in! The Father Marquette Shrine boat ramp is on your right.

The Suttons Landing to Father Marquette Shrine crack research team: Spencer Vollmers, Jimmy Vollmers, Eric Braun, Paul "Colonel" Braun, Ronnie Swiecki Jr., Ron Swiecki, Juan Shell, and Doc

S. S. Badger Car Ferry – Ludington

To paraphrase the Taco Bell Chihuahua, "I think we need a bigger boat"…

You've canoed and kayaked the entire 65 miles of the Pere Marquette River, taking it west from its headwaters near Baldwin to its river mouth ending as it empties into Lake Michigan. Before continuing westward and crossing the Big Lake, you may want to consider switching to a larger craft, trading your canoe/kayak for a ride on the majestic car ferry, S. S. Badger.

The *S. S. Badger* is a wonderful way to travel across Lake Michigan. It is the largest car ferry to ever traverse the Big Lake. The ship is 410' long and 7 stories high. If John Pinette was a boat, he'd be the Badger, as the ship weighs in at a staggering 6,650 tons!

To cross the 60 miles from Ludington to Manitowoc, Wisconsin (south of Green Bay and north of Milwaukee), the journey on the *S.S. Badger* takes approximately 4 hours. There are few feelings as cool as standing on the big boat's forward deck, the wind whistling through your hair, when the harbor first comes into view near the trip's end.

The *S. S. Badger* first went into service in 1953, primarily to transport railroad freight cars. As the need for such a service slowly died out, the Badger made what appeared to be its final voyage, ending up in Ludington, in November of 1990. Businessman Charles Conrad purchased the ship, and remodeled and marketed the *S. S. Badger* to carry leisure passengers and their vehicles. Ready to roll in 1991, the "new" *S. S. Badger* was an immediate hit, creating happiness for travelers on a daily basis from mid-May to mid-October each year.

There's something pretty neat about playing a game of pinball while Lake Michigan churns beneath you. Besides the game room, the ship features a deli-style snack bar, indoor seating, free movies, TV lounges, museum, kid's playroom, private staterooms, ship store and gift shop, and outdoor deck areas.

As you disembark the *S. S. Badger,* you may find yourself quoting Jimmy Buffett, "We bid our farewell much too soon. Honey, it's been a lovely cruise."

The *S. S. Badger* is in port on Pere Marquette Lake. P.M. Lake connects Pere Marquette River to Lake Michigan. In Ludington, take US10 (Ludington Street) to James Street. Go south on James until it ends at the Ludington Dock. Their address is 701 Maritime Drive, Ludington MI 49431. Phone (231) 845-5555. Website www.ssbadger.com.

Father Jacques Marquette Shrine aka "the Cross"

On the south side of Ludington, along the western shore of Pere Marquette Lake, is a shrine to Father Jacques Marquette (in French, Father is Pere), the man who is the namesake of the Pere Marquette River, Pere Marquette Lake, and various towns, townships, counties, and universities.

Father Marquette was a French Jesuit missionary who lived from 1637 to 1675. He and his fellow Jesuits founded Sault Ste Marie in 1668 and St. Ignace in 1671, the 2nd and 3rd oldest European settlements in the Midwest. Built in tribute to the spot where most historians believe that Father Marquette died, the shrine features a tall white cross sitting upon on a hill in the Buttersville Peninsula along South Lakeshore Drive.

Pere Marquette River paddlers may reach the shrine by launching at Sutton's Landing and following the P.M. current as it flows west to the eastern edge of Pere Marquette Lake. Once in the lake and continuing westbound, you cruise past the car ferry S.S. Badger on your right. Looking straight ahead presents you with your first glimpse of "the Cross". Since burned down and replaced with the metal cross that you see today, the original wood cross was said to have inspired the hymn "Old Rugged Cross".

Besides being an intrepid explorer and founder of the Michigan settlements noted earlier, Father Marquette was a caring teacher to, and learned the language of, the indigenous people. The Native Americans in turn loved him and asked Marquette to teach their fellow tribesmen located to the south. They told Father Marquette of a great river that would take him to their kin, and they called the river Misi-Ziibi, Ojibwa for "Giant River" and the origin of the Mississippi River's name.

On May 17, 1673, Father Marquette, with fellow explorer Louis Jolliet and their small party of voyageurs, put two birch bark canoes into Lake Michigan in the U.P. town of St. Ignace. They then paddled west across the northern edge of the big lake, taking it into the waters of Green Bay where they located the river mouth of Wisconsin's Fox River. Canoeing against the current of the Fox, they paddled to the town of Portage, where they performed a task that gave the town its name – they portaged over land for two miles from the Fox to the Wisconsin River. Now moving with the current, Marquette and Jolliet canoed down the Wisconsin River until it flowed into the Misi-Ziibi, or Mississippi, River. Following the Mississippi's current south, they paddled by later-day St. Louis and Memphis all the way down to the river mouth of the Arkansas River, before retracing their steps back to St. Ignace.

Marquette, Joliet and their band paddled for 4 months, on 2,000 miles of rivers and lakes through unchartered wilderness. During this journey, they became the first Europeans to map the Mississippi, and showed all that there was a water highway that would take you from northern-most Lake Michigan south to the Gulf of Mexico.

In 1674 and 1675, Father Marquette's explorations and missionary work took him to the Illinois territory where he built the first European dwelling in what is now Chicago. In early 1675, a bout of dysentery, contracted from his adventure along the Mississippi 2 years earlier, overtook him. On May 18, 1675, while attempting to make it back to his beloved St. Ignace, Father Jacques Marquette died near the shores of Lake Michigan by present-day Ludington. He was 38 years old.

Two of Marquette's traveling companions buried him near the site of where the cross today stands. Pere Marquette finally made it back to his adopted home two years later: in 1677 his body was moved to St. Ignace. Father Jacques Marquette's grave is now found at the Museum of Ojibwa

Culture on State Street in St. Ignace.

The Father Marquette Shrine ("the Cross") is located at 760 South Lakeshore Drive in Ludington MI 49431. From town, take Pere Marquette Highway 2 miles south from US10. After crossing the P.M. River, turn right (west) on to Iris Road. Take Iris for 1.5 miles to Lakeshore Drive and turn right (north). Follow Lakeshore Drive for 1.6 miles. The memorial will be on your right. The site includes 400' of frontage and a boat launch on Pere Marquette Lake.

Sportsman's Irish Pub

"An Irishman walks out of a bar… no really, it could happen". This outlandish statement is written on the t-shirts that the Pub staff wears. These t-shirts are great, but the bar is better.

The Sportsman's Irish Pub opened in 1955 and sits in a building constructed in the 1890s. The tavern is a comfortable meld of the 1890s, the 1950s, and today, and exudes a certain warmth that makes you want to stay a very long time. The interior is long 'n narrow, and upon entering it's as if you've boarded the party car on an excursion train bound for fun. There are many great pieces to this cool puzzle, but it's above you that your eye is first drawn, to the original tin ceiling in all of its glorious 1890's detail (to see what the rest of the bar looked like in 1890, check out the photograph in the foyer). The "Sportsman's" name on the back bar looks like it could've been there since the place opened in '55, and it is a very cool look.

Bar stools are the seats that greet you when you first walk in, and they are hard to leave once you've found a home on one (to quote John Hiatt, "I was gonna get up off of that bar stool, just as soon as I could figure it out"). However, the gorgeous lighting pulls you further into the Sportsman's, like la petite femme skunk does to Pepe Le Pew. As you stroll deeper into the tavern, passing by the other bar stools on your right and tables on your left, you come to a fork in the road that pulls you strongly in 3 ways…

1.   Straight ahead to a pool table and the beautifully-drawn troll murals adjacent to the table (those trolls are rascals).

2.   Right to an alcove ("the cove" to the staff and regulars) with a long table for eight. Behind it is a Detroit Tigers mirror as long as the table itself.

3.   Left to an inviting side room, about 20' x 20', that would make a fine setting for a private euchre party. The room has 9 sets of tables and chairs, some high-backed, with one of the tables on an elevated area next to a gas fireplace. The ancient phone booth in the right corner seems to fit perfectly.

"Hoyt's Original Wimpy Burger" is the namesake of the man who opened the pub back in 1955, Hoyt Payment. The burger is dee-licious. Condiments on this burger would be a waste. The crinkle fries that come with are very good, too. Terri was the day's bartender, the granddaughter in-law of original owner Hoyt (Hoyt's son Mike runs the tavern these days) and a person who knows the history of the Sportsman's pretty well. Besides sharing the chronology of the changes the pub's structure has gone through, Terri passed along one particularly fun fact of the tavern's board de fare: the Pub was the 1st Ludington establishment to serve pizza (which began in 1963). This fact alone elevates the Sportsman's to revered status among the town's residents and visitors.

The Sportsman's wall sign reads, "Good Times with Good Friends since 1955". Once within these tavern walls, you have no reason to doubt the sentiment's accuracy.

Sportsman's Irish Pub is located on US10 in downtown Ludington, 111 W. Ludington Avenue, (231) 843-2138. Their website is www.sportsmansirishpub.com.

Paddling the P. M. River in 8 days, from headwaters to rivermouth

Day 1 The Forks to Gleason's Landing – 9.5 miles, 3 hours

Day 2 Gleason's Landing to Rainbow Rapids – 10.5 miles, 3 hours & 20 minutes (since the Forks, 20 miles, 6 hours & 20 minutes)

Day 3 Rainbow Rapids to Lower Branch Bridge – 8.5 miles, 2 hours & 45 minutes (since the Forks, 28.5 miles, 9 hours & 5 minutes)

Day 4 Lower Branch Bridge to Walhalla Road Bridge – 8 miles, 2 hours & 40 min. (since the Forks, 36.5 miles, 11 hours & 45 min.)

Day 5 Walhalla Road Bridge to Indian Bridge – 5 miles, 1 hour & 40 min. (since the Forks, 41.5 miles, 13 hours & 25 minutes)

Day 6 Indian Bridge to Scottville Road Bridge – 7.4 miles, 2 hours & 45 min. (since the Forks, 48.9 miles, 16 hours & 10 minutes)

Day 7 Scottville Road Bridge to Sutton's Landing – 12.4 miles, 4 hours & 15 min. (since the Forks, 61.3 miles, 20 hours & 25 min.)

Day 8 Sutton's Landing to Ludington Lighthouse (edge of Lake Michigan) – 3.5 miles, 1 hour & 10 minutes

Total P.M. River length: 64.8 miles, 21 hours & 35 minutes

Pere Marquette River from East to West
Public Accesses, Camping, Restrooms

Day 1

The Forks – the very beginning of the P.M.; the access is 20' downstream from where the Little South Branch merges with the Middle Branch to create the P.M. Take M37 south from Baldwin for 3 miles (you'll pass Baldwin Canoe Rental)) to 76th Street and turn left (east). Take 76th east for one-half mile, passing over the Little South Branch, to James Street and then turn left (north) on to James Street & the access is on your left in .2 of a mile.
Public access – yes, camping – no, restroom - yes

M37 Bridge – access is on the east side of M37, 100' north of and across the street from the Baldwin Canoe Rental livery. Across M37 and 20' north from the access is 72nd Street, which runs west only from M37.
Public access – yes, camping – no, restroom - yes.

Ivan's Canoes, Campgrounds and Cabins – located 2 miles north of the P.M. Ivan's has cabins & 60 camp sites, electrical hookups, showers, camp store, pavilion, horseshoes, flush toilets, playground, and volleyball. Ivan's is at 7332 S. M37 in Baldwin 49304, (231) 745-3361, www.ivanscanoe.com.
Public access – no, camping – yes, restroom - yes

Green Cottage – take 72nd Street for 1.5 miles west of M37 until the pavement ends and turn right on to Peacock Street. Go .3 mile on Peacock to the river. Boat ramp is on the south side of the P.M. This is an extremely popular spot with fishermen and it's almost impossible to find a parking spot anywhere near the P.M. during the late-Sept/early-Oct salmon run. At that time of year, the river here is so crowded with fishermen and their boats that paddlers should opt for a different P.M. segment to float.
Public access – yes, camping – no, restroom - no

Claybanks - from M37 in downtown Baldwin, take Eighth Street west for one-half mile to Astor Road and turn left (south). Follow Astor Road for .7 mile to 56th St and turn right (west). Take 56th Street for .2 mile to Claybanks Road and turn left (south). Once you're on Claybanks Road, in 2.6 miles you see 9 camping sites & multiple restrooms. Claybanks is not a public access point as the riverside hill that it sits upon is very steep (with beautiful wooden steps on the hillside) and a tough place to carry your boats and gear up. Call (231) 745-4631.
Public access – no, camping – yes, restroom - yes

Day 2

Gleason's Landing – from M37 in downtown Baldwin, take Eighth St west for one-half mile to Astor Road and turn left (south). Follow Astor Road to the first right that you come to, 52nd Street. Follow 52nd Street west for 2 miles to S Jenks Road – there is a sign for Gleason's Landing just before 52nd meets S Jenks – and turn left (south) at S Jenks. In .4 mi you hit a split in the road. Take the bend right which puts you on to the aptly named Shortcut Lane. On Shortcut Lane for .4 of a mile you arrive at a stop sign and turn right (west) on to 60th Street. Once on 60th, you drive for .3 of a mile then turn left (south) at S Brooks Road and drive for one-half mile to the P.M.
Gleason's has 4 sites, each with a table & fire ring, and 2 group sites. (231) 745-8760.
Public access – yes, camping – yes, restroom - yes

Bowman Bridge - from M37 in downtown Baldwin, take Eighth St west for one-half mile to Astor Road and turn left (south). Follow Astor Road to the first right that you come to, 52nd Street. Follow 52nd Street west for 2.6 miles (.6 mile past S Jenks) to a split in the road where there is a sign pointing right to Rainbow Rapids (on to Wingleton Road) in 4 miles OR left (as 52nd Street becomes 56th Street) and 2 miles to Bowman Bridge – stay left. Once you cross the P.M., the access is to the right. Bowman has 24 camp sites with tables & fire rings and 4 group sites. Call (231) 745-4631.
Public access – yes, camping – yes, restroom -yes

Day 3

Rainbow Rapids – from M37 in downtown Baldwin, take Eighth St west for one-half mile to Astor Road and turn left (south). Follow Astor Road to the first right that you come to, 52nd Street. Follow 52nd Street west for 2.6 miles (.6 mile past S Jenks) to a split in the road where there is a sign pointing right to Rainbow Rapids (on to Wingleton Road) in 4 miles OR left (as 52nd Street becomes 56th Street) and 2 miles to Bowman Bridge. Follow the split right and on to the dirt of Wingleton Road to get to Rainbow Rapids. After driving for 4.4 miles, and crossing over creeks twice on tree-lined Wingleton Road, turn left and cross immediately over the railroad tracks.
Public access – yes, camping – no, restroom - yes

Sulak – from the town of Branch on US10, take Tyndall Road south (Tyndall is just a few feet west of the Oasis Bar) for one-half mile to Stevenson Road and turn left (east). Stevenson Road will bend right (south) and become S Branch Road. One-half mile south of the P.M. (and the Upper Branch Bridge access) is the left turn on to an unmarked road that takes you to Sulak. The total mileage from US 10 to the unmarked Sulak turn in is 2.7. There are 12 Sulak sites. Call (231) 745-4631.
Public access – yes, camping – yes, restroom - yes

Upper Branch Bridge - from the town of Branch on US10, take Tyndall Road south (Tyndall is just a few feet west of the Oasis Bar) for one-half mile to Stevenson Road and turn left (east). Stevenson Road will bend right (south) and become S Branch Rd. Cross over the P.M. and turn right (west) into the access site. The total mileage from US10 to the river is 2.2 miles.
Public access – yes, camping – no, restroom – yes

Elk - a free "canoe-to-only" (not vehicle accessible) site easily visible from the river. Elk is a 10 minute paddle downstream from the Upper Branch Bridge public access and on your left. It has 4 camp sites each with fire rings & benches.
Public access – yes, camping – yes, restroom - yes

Pere Marquette Campground - from the town of Branch on US10, take Tyndall Road south (Tyndall is just a few feet west of the Oasis Bar) for one-half mile to Stevenson Road & turn left (east). Stevenson Road will bend right (south) and become S Branch Rd. 1 mile south of the P.M. (and the Upper Branch Bridge access) and at the top of a hill, turn right (west) on to 40th Street and the campground is in one-half mile. The nearest river access site is at Sulak, a 1.5 mile drive away. PMC has 40 acres of sites w/ picnic tables & fire pits, cabins, showers, flush toilets, pavilions, & a camp store. When staying at PMC and renting from Baldwin Canoe Rental, BCR will bus you from the campground to the river, and – at the end of the trip – bus you from the river back to the campgrounds. The PMC address is 11713 W. 40th St in Branch MI 49402. Call (231) 898-3511, www.pmcampground.com.
Public access – no, camping – yes, restroom - yes

Day 4

Lower Branch Bridge – one-half mile west of Tyndall Road in Branch, and 3 miles east of Walhalla Road in Walhalla, is Landon Road. Take Landon Rd south from US10 for .7 miles, and the access is just over the river and on the right (west) side of the road.
Public access – yes, camping – no, restroom - no

Day 5

Walhalla Road Bridge – from the town of Walhalla, drive 1.4 mi south of US10 on Walhalla Road, cross the P.M. and turn right (west) to the access.
Public access – yes, camping – no, restroom - yes

Day 6

Indian Bridge – Reek Road is 3.2 miles west of Walhalla Road, and 2 miles east of Custer Road, on US10. Turn south from US10 on to Reek Road. Pass an asparagus farm in .6 of a mile on the right. At 1.2 miles south of US10, cross the bridge over the P.M. and turn right (west). The boat ramp is downstream from the bridge on the river's left (south) bank. On the upstream approach to the bridge, the P.M. has 4 fingers flowing west, merging into one a few feet before the bridge.
Public access – yes, camping – no, restroom – yes

Custer Road Bridge – at Bonser's Market (look for the big cow head sticking out of the building along US10) in downtown Custer, turn south on to Custer Road. In two miles you'll reach the P.M. Cross the bridge and turn left. The access is just upstream from the bridge and on the left (south) bank. No sign announces the access.
Public access – yes, camping – no, restroom – no

Scottville Riverside Park - from US10 in downtown Scottville, take Main Street south as it becomes Scottville Road. The P.M. is one mile south of US10. Just after crossing the river, turn left into the Park. SRP has 50 sites with electricity, water, and cable, plus additional primitive sites. There is a picnic area, playground, bath house, and a large shelter w/ a stone fireplace. SRP is located upstream from the Scottville Road Bridge. The nearest river access is off-site, on the downstream side of the bridge. Call (231) 757-2429, www.scottvilleriversidepark.com.
Public access – no, camping – yes, restroom - yes

Day 7

Scottville Road Bridge – from US10 in downtown Scottville, take Main Street south as it becomes Scottville Road. The P.M. is one mile south of US10. Just before arriving at the river bridge, turn right for the access (the nearest access for campers at Scottville Riverside Park).
Public access – yes, camping – no, restroom - yes

Henry's Landing and Canoe Livery - from US10 in downtown Scottville, take Main Street south as it becomes Scottville Road. The P.M. is one mile south of US10. Immediately after crossing the river, turn right into Henry's, located directly across the river from the Scottville Road Bridge access. Every campsite is along the banks of the P.M., 23 electric and 22 primitive sites. Henry's has a general store and showers. Their address is 701 S. Scottville Road in Scottville 49454. Call (231) 757-0101, www. henryslanding.com.
Public access – yes, camping – yes, restroom – yes

Pere Marquette Highway 31 landing - take US10 in Ludington to the Pere Marquette Highway and turn south. Cross over both the North and the South Branches of the P.M. When you cross the South Branch of the P.M. (1.9 miles south of US10), turn left to the access.
Public access – yes, camping – no, restroom - no

Day 8

Sutton's Landing – take US10 in Ludington to the Pere Marquette Highway and turn south. Crossing over both the North and the South Branches of the P.M., it's 2 miles from US10 to Iris Road (at P.M. Expeditions Beers, Boats & Bait). Turn right (west) at Iris Road. In one-tenth of a mile, the entrance to Sutton's Landing will be on your right. Shelter, picnic tables, park benches, swing set & wooden dock overlook the P.M.
Public access – yes, camping – no, restroom - yes

Buttersville Park - from downtown Ludington, take US10 east to Pere Marquette Highway and turn right (south). Go 2 miles, crossing over the North and South Branches of the P.M., and turn right on to Iris Road. Take Iris for 1.5 miles until it ends at South Lakeshore Drive and turn right (north). It's a little over a mile to Buttersville Park's (3 minutes south of the Father Marquette Shrine) 44 sites each w/ electricity & picnic tables. You'll find restrooms, pavilion, swings 'n slides, showers & flush

toilets.   Many sites on the beautiful shaded grounds have wonderful views of Lake Michigan. Buttersville Park is at 991 S. Lakeshore Drive, Ludington 49431. Call (231) 843-2114.
Public access – no, camping – yes, restroom - yes

Father Marquette Shrine aka "the Cross" - from Sutton's Landing, turn right (west) on to Iris Road and drive 1.5 miles to South Lakeshore Highway. Turn right (north) and drive 1.6 miles to the Father Marquette Shrine, located on the right. The canoe and kayak access is behind the Shrine (the Cross).
Public access – yes, camping – no, restroom - yes

Paddling & Camping Checklist

bug spray
first aid kit
sunglasses
2 sets of vehicle keys
trash bags (for canoes/kayaks & water for campground)
food
knife
bungee cords
zip locks (large & small)
dry clothes (for canoes/kayaks & flashlights for campground)
fire starters & matches/lighters
tent
thermarest/air mattress
nose strips (for snoring friends)
grill & grate
forks/spoons/plates
can opener
dish soap/scrub brush soap
euchre decks
toilet paper
water, soap, flashlights

sun block
rain poncho
dry (waterproof) bags
plastic drop cloths (for rain)
cooler & ice
clothesline rope
baseball cap
towels
river shoes & dry shoes
frisbees
camera
sleeping bag
blankets & pillows
ear plugs (defense if snoring friends)
pots/pans/large spoon
hand towels
tin foil (for grub leftovers)
toothpaste/toothbrush
$$$ & wallet
campsite chairs

Pere Marquette River
Canoe & Kayak Liveries
From East to West

Baldwin Canoe Rental 231-745-4669, 800-272-3642
9117 South M37, P. O. Box 269, Baldwin, MI 49304
sales@baldwincanoe.com
http://www.baldwincanoe.com

Ivan's Canoe Rental 231-745-3361, 231-745-9345
7332 South M-37, Baldwin, MI 49304
 ivanscampground@sbcglobal.net
http://www.ivanscanoe.com

Henry's Landing & Canoe Livery 231-757-0101
701 S. Main Street, Scottville, MI 49454
henryslanding@yahoo.com
http://www.henryslanding.com

River Run Canoe Livery 231-757-2266
600 S Main St., Scottville, MI 49454
http://www.riverruncanoerental.com

Pere Marquette Expeditions/Nelson's Frontier Market, 231-845-7285
1649 South Pere Marquette Hwy, Ludington, MI 49431
pmexpeditions@gmail.com
http://www.pmexpeditions.com

ABOUT THE AUTHOR: DOC FLETCHER

Doc discovered a love of water at an early age. He's pictured here with his Mom (Mary) in Lake Michigan, a bit south of where Father Marquette died in 1675, near the end of the Pere Marquette River's journey. Dad (Herb) is taking the picture.

This is Doc's 5th book published by Arbutus Press. His other books are "Weekend Canoeing in Michigan", "Michigan Rivers Less Paddled", "Canoeing and Kayaking Wisconsin", and "Paddling Michigan's Hidden Beauty"